Speaking and listening
Ages 7–9
Activities in cross-curricular contexts

D1612554

Authors

Eleanor Gavienas,
Deirdre Grogan,
Joyce Lindsay and
Jennifer Logue

Editor

Dulcie Booth

Series Designer

Clare Brewer

Assistant Editor

Roanne Charles

Designer

Clare Brewer

Illustrations

Ray and Corinne
Burrows

Cover Photograph

Martyn Chillmaid

Inside photographs

© Derek Cooknell; Clare
Brewer; Corel; Hulton Getty;
2003 Jorvik; Art Explosion;
Ikon Imaging; Photodisc;
Stock Market; Clara Von Aich/
SODA; Ana Esperanza Nance/
SODA; Richard Hutchings/
SODA; David Franck/SODA;
Paul Aresu/SODA; David
Mager/SODA; Scott Campbell/
SODA; Bie Bostrom/SODA;
Stanley Bach/SODA;
Photodisc via SODA.

Acknowledgements

The publishers gratefully acknowledge permission to reproduce the following copyright material:

Ordnance Survey® for mapping and symbols licensed from Ordnance Survey® with the permission of the Controller of Her Majesty's Stationery Office, © Crown Copyright. All rights reserved. Licence no. 100039768.

Every effort has been made to trace copyright holders for the works reproduced in this book, and the publishers apologise for any inadvertent omissions.
Every effort has been made to ensure that websites and addresses referred to in this book are correct and educationally sound. They are believed to be current at the time of publication. The publishers cannot be held responsible for subsequent changes in the address of a website, nor for the content of the sites mentioned. Referral to a website is not an endorsement by the publisher of that site.

British Library Cataloguing-in-Publication Data
A catalogue record for this book is available from the British Library.

ISBN 0-439-97645-6

Designed using Adobe InDesign

The rights of Eleanor Gavienas, Deirdre Grogan, Joyce Lindsay and Jennifer Logue to be identified as the Authors of this work have been asserted by them in accordance with the Copyright, Designs and Patents Act 1988.

Published by Scholastic Ltd,
Villiers House, Clarendon Avenue,
Leamington Spa, Warwickshire CV32 5PR
www.scholastic.co.uk

Printed by Bell & Bain Ltd, Glasgow

Text © 2004 Eleanor Gavienas, Deirdre Grogan, Joyce Lindsay and Jennifer Logue
© 2004 Scholastic Ltd

1234567890 4567890123

Contents

Introduction	4
Classroom techniques	6
Assessment	18

Units

1 Weather	27
2 Brushing teeth	38
3 Fridge magnets	46
4 Evacuation	54
5 Village settlers	67
6 The Egyptians	82
7 The Vikings	91
8 Our environment	102
9 Chocolate bars	113

Introduction

To operate effectively in social situations children must develop communication skills. Speaking is an important skill in its own right and listening is inextricably linked to it. In the English curriculum speaking and listening are very closely linked to reading and writing. Indeed, reading often leads to speaking and listening, and speaking often leads to writing and therefore back to reading. The four outcomes of language complement each other. Speaking and listening are also vital skills for accessing the curriculum. Children and teachers speak and listen in history, geography, science, maths, RE, PSHE and citizenship. If children can develop effective communication skills they will learn more effectively across the curriculum.

Research over the past 20 years has recognised the contribution speaking and listening makes to learning. Through speaking, children are able to practise and develop many thinking skills – skills of forming their ideas, making their ideas explicit to others, organising and reorganising their ideas. Speaking is not simply about sharing ideas, but it does help children to clarify their thinking and explain their ideas to others.

▌ Importance of context

Most teachers recognise that children learn better when they are interested, motivated and actively engaged. Too often in the past speaking and listening activities have not provided interest and motivation, and have not engaged children because they have been presented as decontextualised exercises with limited purposes. Often these purposes were not shared with, nor understood by, the children. The speaking and listening activities presented in this book will provide motivation because the contexts they are developed around will be of interest to 7 to 9-year-olds, because they are presented in a variety of ways – many of which are collaborative, and because the children will clearly see and understand the purposes of the activities. Setting the speaking and listening activities within a context will:

- encourage children to actively participate in speaking and listening
- interest children and develop their knowledge and skills across the curriculum
- provide real and meaningful purposes for children's talk
- provide audiences which are real
- help children to make links between what they already know and their new learning.

Speaking and listening are outcomes in the language curriculum but it is clear that they are essential skills for learning in all areas of the curriculum. The units chosen in this book present speaking and listening activities within topics currently undertaken in schools at the junior stages in the English National Curriculum for history, geography and science and the Scottish environmental studies 5–14 guidelines for social subjects and science.

▌ Using the activities

The activities within each unit can be used as part of the English programme, during language time or as part of the Literacy Hour or they can be covered during history, geography, science or environmental studies lessons. This allows the teacher some flexibility – a key principle but a threatened one in a crowded curriculum.

Flexibility

Flexibility is also the key to many of the activities. Each unit has a variety of activities. These may require the children to work as a group to brainstorm and create a list of key points, to select or order items from a given list or to come to a consensus as a group. These ideas and ways of structuring and designing tasks can be transferred from one activity to another. An example might be 'Conscience alley' within the Vikings unit (see page 98). This technique could be transferred to any historical context where key characters have difficult decisions to make. For example, Elizabeth I and Mary, Queen of Scots, or evacuation. Similarly for units – the ideas and sequence in one unit may be adapted relatively easily for another. For example, the ideas focusing on persuasive language in 'Chocolate bars' could be used for selling anything in any context.

Class or group work

All of the units provide the opportunity for children to work in both class and group settings and sometimes in pairs. There is an emphasis on group discussion because this is an aspect identified from research as being important for developing children's learning and skills and an area which historically has received little emphasis in the classroom.

At times groups may work on the same task at the same time. At other times and for other activities it may not be necessary or desirable for all groups to work on the same task. Each group may be set a different task and come together for sharing. At times only one group may be involved in collaborative work, with other groups doing the task at a different time or on a different day. All these things will depend on the nature of the task, the experience of the children and the teacher's decisions about organisation. Teachers should remember that it can be counterproductive to insist on all groups reporting back or each group in turn making a presentation. This would not contribute to the positive ethos teachers strive to establish when bringing purposeful and involving speaking and listening activities into the classroom.

Classroom techniques

This book will provide busy teachers with a variety of contextualised activities for the 7–9 age group. However, helping children to speak and listen well will depend on more than provision of activities. Teachers might find some of the following techniques helpful in developing speaking and listening skills in their pupils.

▌ Bringing speaking and listening into the classroom

One of the most vital parts of a teacher's job is to create an ethos which values children's talk. To do this, the teacher needs to engender an atmosphere of trust and security, in which children feel they can take risks in presenting their ideas and feelings to the teacher and other children. A commitment to ensuring that children feel comfortable about talking in the classroom will help you to get the most from the activities in this book.

Encouraging speaking

Whether working with children on a whole-class basis or with a small group, teachers should provide a good model of exploratory talk and questioning. A general aim of this book would be for teachers to encourage children to explore a range of possibilities rather than looking for the correct answer. Adopting the following strategies will help to promote effective interaction between teacher and children:

■ Ask more open questions, for example *Why did you decide on...? How did you go about...?*

■ Increase the length of time you give children to respond after asking a question, in order to give them time to think about their response. This is likely to encourage greater participation and fuller contributions.

■ Use alternatives to questions, such as statements, constructive comments and encouraging gestures. These are often more effective in prompting reflective and extensive responses, for example *I was wondering if... I like your idea about...*

■ Encourage children to say more rather than saying it for them, for example *Tell us a little more about your reason for... Why did you choose that one?*

■ Listen more carefully and for longer periods.

While the techniques explained above are useful in the ways outlined, they only feature explicitly in a limited number of activities. It is the context, task structure and the teaching of specific group interaction behaviour and language which will lead to effective group discussion. Guidance has been given in previous sections in relation to these aspects. However, as with the suggestions for designing tasks, the techniques are useful tools for teachers planning further opportunities for children's involvement in group discussion.

▌ Drama

While drama is well established as a subject in its own right, with its own particular knowledge, skills and attitudes to be developed, it is also acknowledged that children learn effectively *through* drama. Hence the drama activities in the book have been planned into the units, both to extend children's learning in drama and to deepen their understanding of ideas, situations, characters and events. There are also clear links between the drama activities and the other targets in speaking and listening. When children are planning and evaluating their work in drama, this may involve skills in group discussion. Speaking clearly and with attention to the needs of the listeners will also be enhanced through involvement in drama activities. The potential for drama to encourage reflective thinking should not be restricted to the curriculum in English. Opportunities to transfer the techniques described on page 16 should be considered in other curriculum areas.

Use of space
Many of the drama activities included in the book can be undertaken in an average-sized classroom. It is possible to train children at this stage to move classroom furniture quickly and safely to create space to work. There are times when a larger 'performance' space should be used, for example when drama is being presented to others. Indeed, it is valuable experience for children to undertake drama activities in a range of settings. Clearly children will need guidance in how to use spaces of different sizes to develop and present their work.

Teacher's role
As with other targets in speaking and listening, key roles for the teacher are to model the drama skill/technique with the children, and to assess progress in the use of particular drama skills. Guidance is provided for both of these aspects of the teacher's role in relevant activities. In addition to these, a valuable role for the teacher in drama is that of a participant.

Shyer children
For most children at this stage, drama is approached with enthusiasm and is regarded as an enjoyable part of the curriculum. However some children may be reluctant to take on a role and say something in front

of the whole class. A more comfortable situation, initially, may be for shyer children to work in pairs and small groups where possible. It may be some time before these children feel comfortable working on a larger scale and sensitivity should be shown in these circumstances. On the other hand, many quieter children find it easier to contribute in a whole-class drama context when they take on a different persona, the security of the role acting as an enabler.

Range of work

At this stage, children should have opportunities to work in role, present drama to others and respond to performances. Many of the activities in the book provide these opportunities. It is anticipated that time will be built in at the end of the drama activities to review and evaluate progress in groups or with the class. The assessment points will assist teachers and children as they respond to performances.

Drama techniques

The following techniques are suggested.

	What is it?	Useful for	Activity
Role-play	Children take on the role of a character, real or imagined. It is most effective when children have some experience or knowledge of the situations and/or characters. Role-play can be set into many contexts and can be spontaneous or rehearsed.	Encouraging language appropriate to a particular situation, character or period; gaining a different perspective on situations and characters; enabling shyer children to participate.	'Weather forecast presentations', page 31
Hot-seating	One person is in role and is questioned by the class, or by a group, who are usually not in role. The person in the hot-seat could be one of the children, the teacher or a visitor. Their responses should be consistent with the role.	Exploring character and motivation; gaining further information about a character; enhancing role-play.	'Interviewing an evacuee', page 60
Meeting	The children come together, in role, in a meeting to present information, plan action, suggest strategies, and solve problems. The role is usually a demonstration of an attitude or viewpoint. It can be linked to the jigsawing technique used in group discussion.	Getting groups into role easily; allowing the possibility of expert roles; establishing control through the meeting structure.	'Presenting the product', page 116
Documentary	The children present information about a topic. The information should be 'real' but the presentation of it can be undertaken in role.	Encouraging wider research and some measure of factual accuracy; enabling groups to contribute their own interests; raising awareness about different forms of presentation; informing other groups and audiences.	'Cookery demonstration', page 118
Freeze frame	The children select or are given a key moment and make a still picture scene based on it. These can be individual, or linked as a sequence, joined by movement, narration, music, poetry, etc. The still picture can be activated to encourage children to 'come to life' briefly, or individuals in the frame can be encouraged to speak their thoughts.	Introducing the idea of images; encouraging selectivity and economy of expression; promoting discussion about meanings behind actions.	'An evacuee's letter home', page 58
Conscience alley	Also referred to as *Thought tunnel*, the children are formed into two lines between which a character can walk. As the character walks down the 'alley', her/his thoughts are spoken aloud as s/he passes each child. The character may be on their way to an event or may have a difficult decision to make. If the character is faced with a dilemma then the children on one side of the 'alley' could outline thoughts associated with one perspective and the other side could outline thoughts associated with a different perspective.	Examining issues from more than one viewpoint; creating tension; deepening understanding of situations, events and characters.	'To settle or move on?', page 98

Speaking to different audiences

Before planning what you will say, you have to think about your audience. Discuss each point in your groups and take notes.

Audience	Notes/resources
Average age? Does this matter?	
How long could they listen for?	
How quickly, slowly should we speak to keep their interest?	
Are there any words that might not be understood by this audience?	
What visual aids would be helpful to the audience?	
How could we involve them? Perhaps ask them to: listen for certain things; vote; ask questions at the end; predict something; guess something before telling them the answer.	
Should we use standard English? Our own dialect? A mixture?	

Assessment

▍Objectives and assessment

Every activity in this book contains assessment points which are closely related to the speaking and listening objectives for the activity. The objectives are based on Key Stage 2 attainment target descriptors for levels 3–5 (levels B–C, talking and listening outcomes in the English language 5–14 Scottish guidelines) so teachers can feel secure in systematically covering national recommendations. Linking the assessment to these objectives is only sensible. Sharing the objectives in an appropriate way with children will clarify the focus for them.

▍Recording assessment

Not all teacher assessments need to be recorded. Informal incidental assessment is as much a part of good teaching as formal written records. However, when more formal records are needed, busy teachers need recording sheets that have two attributes: they must be practical (easy to use) and useful (give real information about particular aspects of speaking and listening). Open-ended sheets of paper do not address the former and tick lists do not always tackle the latter. The assessment sheets in this book (see pages 23–6) have been designed with practicality and usefulness in mind.

▍Self assessment

Perhaps the ultimate aim in any assessment is to lead people to become more aware of their own strengths and development needs. This is no less true of speaking and listening, but because these skills are very natural, 'taken for granted', children perhaps need support in analysing their skills in a more focused way. The fact that speaking and listening is by nature ephemeral adds to the problem of helping children to reflect on progress in this area.

Children of 7–9 years will need support in thinking about their performance and the simplest way to introduce young children to this idea is to sit with them after an activity and ask them to consider how well they met the objectives, for example, *Today we were trying to listen to others' views. When did you find this easy? Difficult? Why? Such* simple questions will pay dividends in helping children to reflect and to articulate their thoughts so that personal next steps are negotiated. This might be done as a class, with a group, or with individuals, depending on the nature of the speaking and listening activity and the teacher's knowledge of her/his pupils' level of confidence in reflection. Modelling such reflection is a powerful way of reinforcing its place in learning. Children would gain much comfort in hearing their teacher saying something like, *Well, we were supposed to be listening to other's views today but I don't think I did this very well with the group I was in! I'm going to try to talk less and listen more in future. How did this group feel about your work today?*

As speaking and listening becomes more firmly established in classrooms, such reflections will naturally take place after some sessions. However, insisting that all sessions end this way might result in stultifying, formulaic plenaries. The teacher should judge when a more formal reflection session is appropriate. There is also place for children to assess themselves to help them reflect on their progress.

You may find photocopiable page 24 helpful in asking children to assess themselves.

▎ Assessing speaking

The assessment of speaking and listening can be a complex and difficult business, not least because of the fundamental differences between the nature of more formal presentational speaking and group discussions. The former allows children to plan, order and rehearse their thoughts whilst the latter is of a much more exploratory nature and affords children the opportunity to think on their feet and respond to each other's opinions. Given these differences, teachers often find it easier to use different criteria to assess the different types of speaking.

Aspect of speaking

Shape and organisation
▎ relevance of material to topic
▎ relevance of material to listeners
▎ appropriateness of vocabulary
▎ appropriateness of syntax

Delivery
▎ audibility
▎ clarity
▎ pacing
▎ engagement of audience

Logistics
▎ use of visual aids
▎ use of equipment
▎ use of notes
▎ positioning of self and visual aids

Body language
▎ stance
▎ composure
▎ scans audience
▎ facial expression
▎ gestures

children referring to you is to avoid eye contact at all times. Children who do not get eye contact eventually ignore you and this is just what is wanted in this instance! Children of this age group might need a little time to adjust to your different role here.

Photocopiable page 25 should help you in your role in assessing children's speaking and listening in groups.

Assessing drama

Much of the above advice might apply to the assessment of drama where the teacher's necessary presence can distort the children's behaviour. Again, when children become more accustomed to your lack of involvement, your presence will cease to become an inhibiting factor.

The problems associated with the lack of evidence of speaking and listening in groups might also apply to drama. This problem often causes teachers to look for more tangible results from drama activities, for example scripts, diary entries of characters, characters' thought tracking and their use of art work such as masks, drawings of characters or settings and props. Whilst such evidence is useful the drive for evidence should not skew the activities towards the production of tangible but sometimes unnecessary outcomes. Evidence of progress in relation to some aspects of drama might be achieved through taking photographs of still images and tableaux to record children's use of space and gesture. The use of the camera will not be off-putting here as children will already be 'posed' during such drama activities. Photocopiable page 25 might help teachers to assess specific drama objectives. Here the teacher should simply try to describe the child's actions and/or words as appropriate to the technique being taught. Analysis and next steps for each child can be considered later.

Many schools video final drama performances, but there is much merit in also doing this during work in progress. As well as providing the teacher with evidence for assessment, it also allows children the opportunity to view themselves and to seek means of improving on their techniques.

Assessing

Group discussion ☐ Listening ☐ Drama ☑ Speaking ☐ (Please tick)

Date: 26th November   Unit: The Vikings
Specific objective: To remain in character by using appropriate posture and linguistic features.

Name	Actions	Words	Summary
Jim (in hot seat as Viking)	Glared at the questioners! Folded his arms and looked intimidating. Never smiled.	I do not understand your silly question Why do you ask me this? Yeah so what? My people hate that rubbish. You have angered me by asking this	Appropriate posture throughout. Obviously recognises aspects of register, eg no contractions. Only few uses of inappropriate vocabulary, eg 'yeah', 'rubbish.
Rizwana	Leaned forward and used her notes well. Appeared to listen well and nodded appropriately. Remained serious-looking throughout	Tell me, Halvar, why do you think... We do not mean to dishonour you when we ask...	Remained in character throughout. Posture and language very appropriate.
Karen	Appeared embarrassed and looked to audience many times Hid face behind clipboard. Giggled a lot. Did not look at Halvar directly.	So tell me Halvar.... Why did your people... That's cool. Thanks	Found it difficult to get into character. Generally used appropriate vocabulary and only slipped towards the end.
Next steps:	Jim: Show him quotes and ask him to circle inappropriate vocabulary. Rizwana: Invite her to be in the hot-seat. Karen: Try similar activity with only 2 or 3 other pupils to reduce embarrassment.		

Talk diary

Keep a talk diary to record your involvement in speaking and listening activities:

▌ Decide whether the main focus for the activity is **speaking**, **listening**, **group discussion** or **drama**.

▌ Write down and complete the two starter sentences below that are linked to the focus of the activity.

▌ Add the date to your entry.

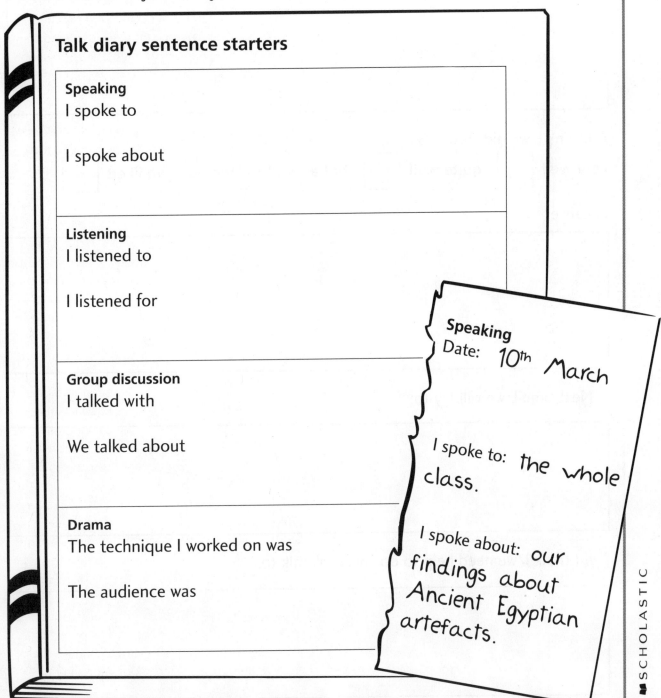

Talk diary sentence starters

Speaking

I spoke to

I spoke about

Listening

I listened to

I listened for

Group discussion

I talked with

We talked about

Drama

The technique I worked on was

The audience was

Speaking

Date: 10th March

I spoke to: the whole class.

I spoke about: our findings about Ancient Egyptian artefacts.

Self-assessment

Name: _____
Date: _____

▮ This activity was about: (Please tick)

Group discussion ☐ **Listening** ☐ **Drama** ☐ **Speaking** ☐

▮ During the activity I was trying to practise the way I/we:

```
[                                                    ]
```

▮ I think I/we did this: (Please tick)

very well ☐ **quite well** ☐ **not as well as I would have liked** ☐

because:

```
[                                                    ]
```

▮ Next time I/we will try to:

```
[                                                    ]
```

▮ If I think I/we need help to do this I will talk to:

```
[                                                    ]
```

SCHOLASTIC

Photocopiable

Assessing:

Group discussion ☐   Listening ☐   Drama ☐   (Please tick)

Name: _____   Date: _____

Unit: _____

Children in group	Examples of *	Examples of *	Summary

Next steps:

* Teachers should add particular activity objectives here.

SCHOLASTIC

Assessing listening

Date: _____

Unit: _____

Feature \ Name				
Eye contact				
Body language				
Asks questions during/after activity				
Makes direct reference to what has been heard				
Applies new knowledge to related activity				

Not all the categories will be appropriate to all listening activities and sources (for example, radio, live presenter, audio tape, video). It might be best to asterisk those categories that will be the focus for each assessment. For some features you may wish to simply tally to denote frequency. For others a brief comment about consistency or quality may be required. In other cases a direct quote or description of response may be helpful.

Weather

Linked to
The National Curriculum for geography, Key Stage 2; Scottish environmental studies 5–14 guidelines, social subjects, 'People and place'

Activity	speaking	listening	group discussion	drama
1. The holidaymakers photocopiable page 34	▌speak audibly and clearly ▌choose material that is relevant	▌ask relevant questions ▌respond to others		
2. Planning a weather report photocopiable pages 35 and 36		▌identify features of language used for a specific purpose ▌recall and re-present important features	▌make relevant contributions ▌take up and sustain different roles	
3. Weather forecast presentations	▌evaluate speech ▌gain and maintain the response of different audiences			▌explore characters and issues ▌create, adapt and sustain different roles
4. Researching the weather photocopiable page 37		▌ask relevant questions ▌recall and re-present important features	▌make relevant contributions ▌qualify or justify ▌deal politely with opposing views	

Planning a weather report

Objectives
▮ To talk in groups to reach a decision

▮ To chose appropriate syntax and vocabulary to suit a given audience

You will need
▮ Large wall map of Britain

▮ Atlases of Britain

▮ Photocopiable pages 35 and 36

▮ A video of a weather forecast for Britain which shows symbols to depict weather conditions (if possible)

▮ Video camera (optional)

Activity time
30 minutes

Assessment
▮ Did children choose, amend or adapt their vocabulary and syntax for given audiences?

▮ Did they come to a group decision?

Background information
Most children will have seen TV weather forecasts. This activity will draw attention to the style used in such oral presentations. It will help children to examine the syntax and vocabulary used in presentations for different audiences.

What to do
Discuss the features of a TV weather report (or if possible play a video of one). These might include the use of symbols, a map of Britain or local area, a presenter, satellite photographs. Draw attention to the types of phrases used in weather forecasts (referring to photocopiable page 36 if appropriate). Explain to the children that they are going to make their very own weather forecast, lasting one to two minutes.

Put the children into groups of three and issue photocopiable page 35. How many of the weather symbols can they name? Discuss the fact that symbols have to be very simple and readily identifiable. Ask the groups to discuss and agree on their own symbols for fog, hailstones, drizzle and heavy rain.

Children should now cut out and, if appropriate, colour the symbols. When they have done this, issue all groups with photocopiable page 36. Ask the children to note only five of the eight weather symbols from photocopiable page 35 to describe the weather over Britain in one day. They should now plan their presentation, using photocopiable page 36. Encourage the children to consider their audience and to try to work systematically through regions. You might want to allot each group a particular audience, for example all adults, all children, families going on holiday in the UK, gardeners. Provide them with atlases to help them to decide on the five regions to highlight. Explain that they should now match the weather condition to the region.

When they are ready to script their presentation, draw the children's attention to the opening sentences and useful phrases on the sheet. Encourage them to mix, match and amend these to suit their weather report. Explain that the choice of language will depend on their audience. Allow children time to plan their script. See the next activity for performing the presentations.

Simplifying the activity
▪ Omit the different audiences aspect and simply tell children that the forecast will be for adults and children.

Extending the activity
▪ Allow children to describe the weather for more than five regions.

Weather forecast presentations

Background information
This activity provides children with the opportunity to present their weather reports.

What to do

Explain to the children that they are going to present their weather reports. Let them have plenty of time to rehearse their presentations. Tell the children that each weather presentation will need one person to give the 'voiceover' or be the reader while another person indicates the weather conditions on a map of Britain. There will also be a director offering the presenter advice on stance and movements and to the reader on clarity and pace. Each group of three must decide who will undertake each role.

Emphasise the need for the reader to use a measured pace to allow the audience to assimilate the information and also for the presenter placing the symbol on the map sufficient time to do this. You may want to model reading aloud a mock weather forecast at a variety of paces to ascertain with the children which might be the most appropriate. Explain that the reader also has to ensure that the pace is responsive to the needs of the presenter, for example if s/he is having difficulty placing a symbol, the reader should stop and wait before moving on. This responsiveness will mean that readers have to lift their heads from their scripts to look at the presenter. Remind presenters that listening carefully and responding to the pace of the reader will be their main concern. Again you may want to model these points. Allow time for the groups to practise using the props (the map and weather symbols).

When the children feel ready to begin, split the class into groups of twelve (four of the trios). Tell the class that when each group presents, their audience should take notes on the weather information gathered. Remind children that when note-taking they can use abbreviations and should not write in sentences.

Each trio should now deliver their presentations, with the director at the side to help out in cases of emergency! After the presentations, the groups can check the accuracy of their notes.

Simplifying the activity

■ Undertake one of the roles yourself within a group.

Extending the activity

■ Let children give feedback under headings they have devised themselves.

Objectives
▌ To pace their reading of a script appropriately

▌ To listen and observe a presentation, taking notes

You will need
▌ Large wall map of Britain

▌ The weather symbols from the previous activity

▌ The children's weather reports from the previous activity

Activity time
30 minutes

Assessment
▌ Did the readers and presenters try to work in tandem?

▌ Did the audience listen and note-take effectively?

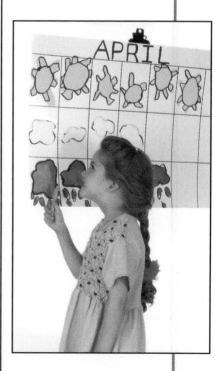

The holidaymakers

■ Match each child to a suitable holiday destination.

Weather symbols

▌ What kind of weather are these symbols representing?

▌ Draw your own weather symbols.

fog	hailstones
drizzle	heavy rain

■SCHOLASTIC

Planning a weather report

▌ The audience for our weather forecast is

_____

▌ We have chosen the following five weather conditions:

_____   _____

_____   _____

_____

▌ We will start (N, S, E or W) _____

▌ We will finish (N, S, E or W) _____

Regions we will focus on	The weather condition will be

Some opening statements	Some useful phrases
Good afternoon, here is the weather forecast brought to you by…	Let's start by looking at…
Hello there and welcome.	When we look at this region, we can see that…
Hiya! If it's weather you want…	If you live in…, you can expect…
Here is the weather forecast for tomorrow.	The best of the weather will be in…
So you want to know what the weather will be like?	If we move on now to…, you can see that…

Researching the weather

	Fog	Sun	Rain	Wind	Snow	Thunder and lightning
Which month/s does this occur most in Britain?						
What causes this to happen?						
A record-breaking fact						
Problems that extremes of this can cause						

Linked to
The National Curriculum for science, Key Stage 2, 'Life processes and living things'; Scottish environmental studies 5–14 guidelines, science,'Living things and the processes of life'

Brushing teeth

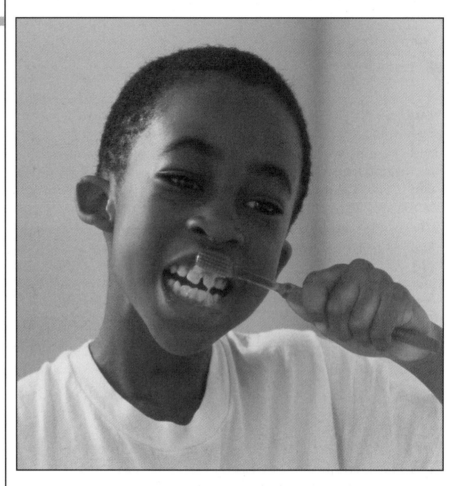

Activity	speaking	listening	group discussion	drama
1. Brushing observation photocopiable page 43	▌speak audibly and clearly ▌use appropriate vocabulary and syntax	▌ask relevant questions ▌identify gist/ key points		
2. Toothbrush test photocopiable page 44		▌respond to others	▌make relevant contributions ▌qualify or justify ▌help the group to move forward	
3. Toothpaste names photocopiable page 45		▌respond to others	▌make relevant contributions ▌explore ideas and evaluate contributions	

Brushing observation

Background information
As well as being a structured opportunity for speaking and listening, this activity provides contextualised opportunities for functional writing – taking brief notes, and for reading for information. Depending on accessibility to resources and the availability of adult supervision, the tooth-brushing part of the activity may be best undertaken in pairs, a group at a time. However, the remainder of the activity could be undertaken with the whole class in pairs.

What to do
Issue the top half of photocopiable page 43 to each child. Go over the questions, explaining to the children that they are going to observe how their partners brush their teeth. Demonstrate how to take brief notes about what they might see, and where to make these notes – in the column *What my partner does*. Explain that they do not need to write anything down in the other column yet. Organise the children into pairs and direct them to undertake their observations – one child brushing, the other child observing. Stop the pairs after a few minutes and tell them to swap roles.

Issue the bottom half of the sheet. Read the questions and recommendations, establishing that the questions are essentially the same as the ones used during the observations. Ask the children to compare what their partner did against the recommendations, writing some brief advice for each question in the last column on the top half of the sheet. For example, if a child has noted *a lot* for the amount of toothpaste used, the advice might be *Use less* or *Use a pea-sized amount*. Give the children about ten minutes for this.

Next, tell the children that they will take it in turns to provide each other with information about tooth brushing techniques based on the observations and notes they made. Model how to do this using notes that one or two of the children have made, for example, *You brushed up and down and my advice would be to brush in a circular motion. You only brushed the outside of your teeth. My advice would be to remember to brush the inside too.* Demonstrate how to listen to the information and how to ask questions for clarification: *Does that mean brush round like this? How should I hold my brush to get behind my front teeth?*

Simplifying the activity
■ Put the children into groups of three – one brushing, one timing, one observing and making notes.

Extending the activity
■ Ask the children to take notes while their partners provide feedback.

Objectives
▌ To provide information based on a structured observation

▌ To listen to information, asking questions to clarify procedures

You will need
▌ Toothbrushes and toothpaste

▌ Timers

▌ Photocopiable page 43 cut in half as indicated

Activity time
1 hour

Assessment
▌ Were children able to use notes from their observation to provide information to their partner?

▌ How effectively did children listen to information, asking questions to clarify procedures?

Toothbrush test

Objectives
▌ To agree a plan for investigation

▌ To use different ways of moving the discussion on

You will need
▌ A selection of toothbrushes (focus on the range designed for children)

▌ Photocopiable page 44

Activity time
45 minutes

Assessment
▌ How successfully did children agree a plan for investigation?

▌ Were children able to use some of the strategies outlined to move the discussion on?

Background information
In order to help children to be more objective and to avoid any child being singled out in relation to the condition of their toothbrush, a selection of new and varied toothbrushes should be used for this activity. Ideally the children would be taken to shop for these, but where this is impractical a set of toothbrushes should be given to a group for investigation.

What to do
First, work with the class to establish key features of toothbrushes. Point out the head, the handle, bristles and so on. Put the children into groups of four or so and provide each group with a set of toothbrushes and photocopiable page 44 for each child. Ask the groups to investigate the toothbrushes, making notes against the recommended features on the sheet. Point out that they will need to decide how to approach this. You may wish to model phrases such as, *Why don't we look at one toothbrush at a time for all the features? Would it be better if we talked about the bristles for all the toothbrushes? If we do, note down all the names of the toothbrushes first then we could look at...*

After about 15 to 20 minutes, direct the children's attention to the 'Other features' aspect at the bottom of the table on the photocopiable page. Collate a list of what these might include, for example bristles change colour after prolonged use, angled handle, rubber grip, image of a popular character. Tell the group that they should examine each of the toothbrushes for such features and make notes on the photocopiable page. They will then make a group decision about which of the toothbrushes they would recommend to others. Before the group actually undertakes this part of the activity, model some of the ways in which they might move the discussion on and achieve a joint decision. For example, *I think we should decide between the ones that have all the recommended features. What do you think ___ (inviting a quieter group member by name)? Do you think we have discussed this one long enough? We only have ten more minutes, maybe we should move onto the next one. We agreed that we wouldn't recommend ones that didn't have... So, it looks like we are going for this one because it has...* Bring the class together firstly, to compare their recommendations and secondly, to review some of the strategies they used to keep the discussion moving along.

Simplifying the activity
▒ Provide fewer toothbrushes for comparison.

▒ Ask children to examine toothbrushes for recommended features only.

Extending the activity
▒ Ask each group to write to a manufacturer of one of the less popular toothbrushes with recommendations for improvement.

Toothpaste names

Background information
Before undertaking this activity, ask children to save and bring in the boxes of the toothpastes they use. You may also want to take note of names of toothpastes before undertaking this activity.

What to do

Ask the children what toothpastes they use. Who chooses the toothpaste to buy – the children or their parents? Do parents use the same toothpaste as they do? What do the children like/dislike about their toothpastes? What colour is their toothpaste? Do they think that some toothpastes will be better than others in cleaning their teeth? Does taste matter? List the names of toothpastes they use on the board and the number of children who use them by each one.

Look closely at the names of toothpastes. Add others here that the children have not included. Are there some similarities here? Do any have *dent* in them? What word does this remind them of? (For example, dentist.) Explain that *dent* refers to teeth. What do the other names make them think of? Take one of the names that does *not* appeal to the children and tell them that they will make a new name for that toothpaste. They can then write to the manufacturer with their ideas.

Distribute photocopiable page 45 to groups and explain that they should discuss each name in turn, using their dictionaries if in doubt about the meaning of the word. They can also add other names of their own. Tell them to first note their own opinions. They should then refer to their notes to offer this opinion to the group. Everyone should note all ideas about the images the name suggests before deciding to accept or reject it. The children should now decide which of the accepted ones are more suitable for children and which are best for adults. Which market do they think the manufacturers are trying to sell to: children or adults? The children should now choose their favourite name for that market.

After ensuring that children understand the task, tell them that you will be expecting them to offer their opinions clearly and to listen courteously to everyone else's suggestions. Explain that you will be listening

Objectives
▌ To offer opinions clearly

▌ To listen courteously to others' opinions

You will need
▌ Dictionaries

▌ Photocopiable page 45

Activity time
30 minutes

Assessment
▌ Did children offer their opinions clearly by referring to their notes?

▌ Did children show that they had listened by the responses they made to others' opinions?

for encouraging comments like, *Yes I agree with you, it does make us think of... That's interesting, I hadn't thought of it that way. I've changed my mind after listening to you.* However, the children should also be aware that they can courteously disagree too, by using phrases such as, *Your idea is good but I still think of... when I hear that word. I agree that it makes us think of good things but I just don't like the sound of the word.*

Before hearing the children's conclusions, it might be worthwhile to tell children how often you heard them using the above phrases and which groups did this particularly well. Ask children if they found it strange using such phrases. If they did, reassure them that this is to be expected at first but that it will become easier with practice. You might also want to ask the children if they remembered to refer to their notes during the discussion.

When all groups have reached a conclusion, ask a spokesperson from each group to present their chosen name and give their reasons. Decide as a class whether to send all recommendations to the manufacturer or to send only one name.

Compose a letter to the toothpaste manufacturer in shared writing. Ask one child to copy this, and send the letter off.

Simplifying the activity
■ Give fewer choices for names.
■ Sit with a group who may have difficulty listening and responding positively to model the talk.

Extending the activity
■ Undertake a survey of each group's final choices, with either all adults or another class in the school, to decide which new name will be offered to the manufacturer. Ask children in their groups to plan a recording sheet for this survey.

Tooth-brushing techniques

What I am looking for	What my partner does	What my advice is
1. How long does s/he brush for?		
2. How much toothpaste does s/he use?		
3. Which direction does s/he brush in?		
4. Which areas of the teeth are brushed?		
5. How is the toothbrush held?		

Toothbrushing techniques

1. How long should s/he brush for? 2–3 minutes.

2. How much toothpaste should s/he use? A pea-sized amount.

3. Which direction should s/he brush in? In a circular direction, with small, scrubbing movements.

4. Which areas of the teeth should be brushed? The outer surfaces of each tooth, upper and lower, then the inside surfaces of each tooth, upper and lower, then, the chewing surfaces of each tooth, upper and lower.

5. How should the toothbrush be held? With the bristle tips held at a 45° angle against the gumline.

Did you know that brushing your tongue helps to freshen your breath?

Toothbrushes

Toothbrush / Features				
Toothbrush head size: ■ small				
Type of bristles: ■ soft ■ round-ended				
Type of handle: ■ wide ■ medium length ■ with thumb ridge				
Other features, for example colour-change bristles, angled handle, rubber grip				

We would recommend the _____ toothbrush because it has _____

It also has _____

New names for toothpaste

Names	Makes us think of...	✔ or ✘	Children or adults?
Smile			
Gloss			
Shine			
Lustre			
Polish			
Twinkle			
Sheen			
Sparkle			
Dazzle			
Gleam			
Pearls			

This group will recommend the name _____ to the manufacturer because _____

_____

Linked to
The National Curriculum for
science, Key Stage 2, 'Physical
processes';
Scottish environmental studies
5–14 guidelines, science, 'Energy
and forces'

Fridge magnets

Activity	speaking	listening	group discussion	drama
1. Sorting fridge magnets photocopiable page 51		▌ ask relevant questions ▌ respond to others	▌ make relevant contributions ▌ qualify or justify ▌ help the group to move forward	
2. What can your magnet hold? photocopiable page 52		▌ ask relevant questions ▌ respond to others	▌ make relevant contributions ▌ qualify or justify ▌ deal politely with opposing views	
3. Customising fridge magnets photocopiable page 53		▌ identify features of language used for a specific purpose	▌ qualify or justify ▌ help the group to move forward	

Sorting fridge magnets

Background information
It would be useful to undertake some teaching, or consolidation, of work on information handling in relation to *tree diagrams* before children begin work on this activity. Depending on the resources available, this activity may be best undertaken a group at a time. With parents' agreement, children could be encouraged to bring in any fridge magnets available from home.

What to do
Put the children into groups and issue each group with an enlarged tree diagram from photocopiable page 51 and a collection of fridge magnets. Explain to the groups that they should consider each of the three questions about the shape, size and position of the magnet in relation to each of the fridge magnets. Demonstrate this to the children using one of the magnets. Then model how they should work together in their group to sort the fridge magnets and reach a consensus. Model phrases such as, *I think this magnet should go up this branch because… What do you think, Fiona? I'm not sure we've put this magnet in the right place. Can someone explain why it should go there? So, everyone agrees that the magnets in Set 3 are…* Undertake a further example with the children, focusing more this time on modelling ways of building on the contributions of others. For example, *I partly agree with David that this set of magnets is…, but it is also… Did you mean that we should put this one here because…?*

Once the groups have sorted the magnets into sets, ask them to interpret this information by describing each set and recording this on the bottom half of photocopiable page 51. Remind them about some of the language they should use to help them to reach a consensus about each set.

It would be helpful for the organisation of the next activity if the sets of magnets were collected in labelled boxes or bags. This could be undertaken as an additional speaking and listening activity, with groups reaching consensus as to which box or bag to place their magnets.

Simplifying the activity
■ Provide multiple copies of labels, such as *circular, non-circular, large, small, centre, not in centre,* to help children describe each set.
■ Provide some adult support.

Extending the activity
■ Children who are very familiar with tree diagrams may be able to cope with additional 'branches', such as *heavier than a £1 coin.*

Objectives
▍ To establish a consensus

▍ To build on others' contributions

You will need
▍ A varied collection of fridge magnets

▍ Photocopiable page 51 (top half separated and enlarged)

Activity time
45 minutes

Assessment
▍ Could children establish a consensus by acknowledging ideas of others in the group?

▍ To what extent were children able to build on each other's contributions?

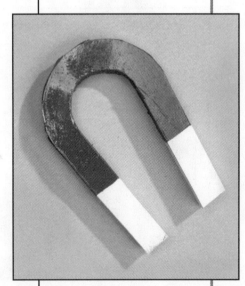

What can your magnet hold?

Objectives
▮ To agree procedures for a fair test

▮ To reach conclusions based on test results

You will need
▮ A collection of fridge magnets

▮ Magnet boards

▮ Sheets of paper, postcards, plastic library cards

▮ Photocopiable page 52

Activity time
45 minutes

Assessment
▮ How successfully did children agree procedures for a fair test?

▮ Were children able to reach conclusions based on test results?

Background information
Depending on the resources available, this activity may be best undertaken a group at a time. However, as groups only need to test one magnet from each set, it may be possible, resource-wise, to have the whole class working in groups for this activity.

What to do
Tell the children that they are going to be testing some fridge magnets to see how effective they are at keeping things in place. Put the children into groups and issue them with a fridge magnet from each set in the previous activity, a magnet board, four sheets of paper, a postcard, a plastic library card and photocopiable page 52.

Discuss with children how they might agree procedures for a fair test. Model the following phrass to the children as a strategy to help them to reach agreement in their group. For example, *Why don't we try all the magnets with one piece of paper first? Should we test one magnet at a time or…? Would it be better if we put the magnet at the top of the paper? Maybe we should see if they could hold more than three sheets of paper.* Once they have decided on their approach, direct each group to undertake their tests and remind them to keep track of their results on the sheet, using a simple tick or cross recording system.

Stop the groups once they have tested a magnet from each set and explain how they should use their results to reach conclusions.

Outline some helpful questions and statements that children may then use, for example, *So, if we look at our table, the only magnet which could hold… was… Were the bigger magnets always better? It looks like all the magnets could… because we have ticks all the way down. Were any of the magnets able to hold…?* Ask the children to summarise their group's discussion by writing concluding sentences on the best and worst magnets. Undertake a class plenary session comparing the groups' results. Children may notice that some differences in results may be due to the weight of the front of the fridge magnet.

Simplifying the activity
▰ Provide children with a simplified version of photocopiable page 52 with fewer things to test for.

Extending the activity
▰ Take the investigation further by encouraging children to weigh the fridge magnets to establish whether this has any effect on their performance.

Customising fridge magnets

Background information
This activity involves children designing and making fridge magnets to suit the likes and hobbies of given customers.

What to do
Divide the class into groups of four or so and issue each group with a selection of fridge magnets. Tell them that later they will decide which of these would be best for particular customers that you are about to describe. Tell children that as you read the descriptions they should listen and take notes of any key words or phrases that might help them decide which magnet would suit each customer. Issue the children with blank paper and ask them to copy the following headings: *Customer's name, Age, Hobbies/likes*. This will help them to take notes.

Customer's name	Age	Hobbies/likes
Anna	7	Listening to music, singing, playing guitar, dancing, soft toy animals

It might be best to revise the note-taking skills of writing only key words and phrases and using abbreviations. Read the description of Anna on photocopiable page 53 and ask the children what they have noted about her. Would any of the fridge magnets they have in front

Objectives
▌ To listen for specific information and take appropriate notes

▌ To refer to notes to help the discussion move forward

▌ To justify decisions by citing of evidence

You will need
▌ Fridge magnets

▌ Photocopiable page 53

▌ Centimetre-squared paper

Activity time
1 hour 10 minutes

Assessment
▌ Were children's notes effective?

▌ How often did children refer to their notes to back up assertions?

of them be to her liking? Discuss other possible objects that might be depicted on a fridge magnet specially made for Anna. Encourage the children to justify their decisions by referring to their notes. Model the kind of talk that you want to hear from children, for example, *I agree with you because I also noted that… I disagree because… When I look at my notes I see that… What had you noted that made you think that?* You may want to note these phrases on the board and tell the children that you want to hear similar phrases during the group discussions. Decide as a class which object would be best depicted on Anna's fridge magnet.

Now tell the children that they will have to decide on suitable fridge magnets for other characters. Read each customer description to the class slowly enough for the children to take notes individually. Then give the groups time to discuss which of the fridge magnets in their collection would be suitable for these customers. Remind them that you will be listening to them referring to their notes when justifying their opinions.

Now allocate a customer from photocopiable page 43 to each group. (It doesn't matter that two groups may have the same customer, as the products will be different.) Explain that they are going to design a customised fridge magnet. Issue the squared paper and ask pairs of children to design a fridge magnet that has no more than three colours and an area no bigger than nine centimetres. When the pairs have designed their magnets, they should join with another pair in their group to compare designs, explaining why theirs would be suitable for their customer. Display these designs.

Simplifying the activity
■ Omit the designing of the fridge magnets.
■ After reading each description, ask children if they would like any parts to be re-read.

Extending the activity
■ It might be fun to ask other teachers or friends and family to write descriptions of their likes and hobbies to send to children for this activity. Children could then send the designs to the adults for comment.
■ Ask the children to make their fridge magnets from modelling clay.

Sorting fridge magnets

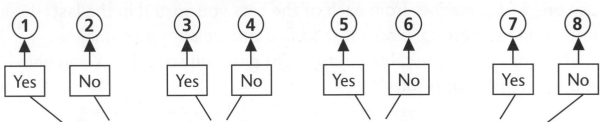

Is the magnet in the centre of the fridge magnet product?

Is the magnet larger than a 5p coin?

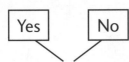

Is the magnet circular?

Start

Once your group has sorted the magnets, discuss how you could describe the magnets in each set. The first set is done for you.

▍ **Set 1:** circular, larger than a 5p coin, in the centre of the magnet holder.

▍ **Set 2:** _____

_____

▍ **Set 3:** _____

_____

▍ **Set 4:** _____

_____

▍ **Set 5:** _____

_____

▍ **Set 6:** _____

_____

▍ **Set 7:** _____

_____

▍ **Set 8:** _____

_____

The strongest magnet holder

Use one fridge magnet from each of the sets you sorted in the last activity. In your group, plan a test to find out which type of magnet holds things best. The table below might give you some ideas and help you to record your results.

Type of magnet	Held a sheet of paper	Held 3 sheets of paper	Held a postcard	Held a library card
1. circular, large, centre				
2. circular, large, not in centre				
3. circular, small, centre				
4. circular, small, not in centre				
5. not circular, large, centre				
6. not circular, large, not in centre				
7. not circular, small, centre				
8. not circular, small, not in centre				

Photocopiable

The customers

Anna

Anna is seven. She has a delightful singing voice and loves listening to all kinds of music. She only has to hear a song once and can remember it. She is learning to play guitar. Her dad plays guitar too, and Anna hopes one day to play with him at events. She also loves dancing and goes to disco, tap and jazz classes. She likes the shows her dance teacher organises, and she wants to make her own costumes one day. Anna has a huge collection of soft toy animals, particularly cats. She wants to be a vet when she is grown up.

Ms Bagla

Ms Bagla is a busy salesperson. She sells all kinds of cars and knows a lot about them. She is very proud of her red sports car. She washes and polishes it every Sunday. Ms Bagla likes to go to the cinema and particularly enjoys computer animation films. She also enjoys computer games and spends at least three hours a week playing these at home. The love of her life is Dandy, her white poodle. Dandy is a cheeky pup who takes her owner for walks in the park!

Mr Cross

Mr Cross is a proud grandfather who loves to go walking with his four-year-old grandson, Daniel. Mr Cross is a keen gardener and planted a birch tree in his garden when Dan was born. He has many plants and flowers, but loves his prize-winning roses best. He has always enjoyed baking and recently started to bake cakes for special occasions. He made a dinosaur-shaped cake for Dan. It looked marvellous, and tasted great too! He often gets requests from friends and family to bake for them.

Lisa

Lisa is a red-haired five year old. She is artistic and is good at putting detail in her pictures. She likes watching her favourite cartoon, *The Little Mermaid*. She adores mermaids. On rainy days Lisa enjoys completing jigsaws, especially ones with mermaids and sea creatures. Like most children, Lisa eats sweets, but would rather eat a Mackintosh Red apple than a chocolate bar! Her mum is delighted about this healthy habit.

SCHOLASTIC

Linked to
The National Curriculum for history, Key Stage 2, 'Britain since 1930';
Scottish environmental studies 5–14 guidelines, social subjects, 'People in the past'

Evacuation

Activity	speaking	listening	group discussion	drama
1. Allocating evacuees photocopiable pages 62 and 63		▌ ask relevant questions ▌ respond to others	▌ make relevant contributions ▌ deal politely with opposing views ▌ help the group to move forward	
2. Packing for evacuation photocopiable page 64		▌ ask relevant questions ▌ respond to others	▌ explore ideas and evaluate contributions ▌ help the group to move forward	
3. An evacuee's letter home photocopiable page 65	▌ speak audibly and clearly ▌ use appropriate vocabulary and syntax	▌ identify features of language used for a specific purpose ▌ respond to others	▌ explore ideas and evaluate contributions ▌ help the group to move forward	
4. Interviewing an evacuee photocopiable page 66	▌ speak audibly and clearly	▌ recall and re-present important features ▌ respond to others	▌ make relevant contributions ▌ qualify or justify ▌ deal politely with opposing views	

Allocating evacuees

Background information
During the Second World War it had been the intention of the authorities that evacuees and 'foster' families would be closely matched to provide a happy and secure environment. However, due to the large numbers being dealt with, evacuees, sadly, were often chosen by the families as if at an auction. This activity provides an insight into how evacuees might have been allocated if time and resources had permitted.

What to do

Provide some background about evacuation in the Second World War. Explain to the children that they are going to work in groups to compile profiles for two sibling evacuees. Compile a sample profile with the class, discussing possible likes and dislikes and so on that imagined evacuees might have. Encourage children to think about personalities. Do the evacuees have a tendency to be quiet/boisterous, tidy/untidy, easily upset/fairly calm? How will they react to being in the countryside away from home. Demonstrate ways of enhancing listening by, for example, scanning the class and making eye contact; inviting class members to contribute; putting forward an idea and giving time for others to respond; acknowledging a good idea; suggesting the use of a popular idea.

In groups of four or so, ask the children to work on the profiles, using the top half of photocopiable page 62. Encourage them to add other important information, referring to the sample profile for ideas.

Once groups have completed the profiles, issue photocopiable page 63. Tell the children to read one family description at a time and discuss advantages and disadvantages would be for each evacuee, based on the profiles they have made. Appoint a scribe for each group to make notes in the second table on photocopiable page 62. Ask the children to do this for all four families.

Before asking the groups to decide on the most suitable/unsuitable family for their evacuees, model how to accommodate views and look for consensus. Ask the children to read the notes they have made on the advantages and disadvantages of each family, then discuss which family is most suitable/unsuitable for their evacuees. They could note this on the back of photocopiable page 62, including reasons.

Simplifying the activity

■ Ask children to create a profile for only one evacuee.

Extending the activity

■ Add another evacuee or family description.

Objectives
▌ To listen to each other's views and preferences

▌ To accommodate different views and look for consensus

You will need
▌ Photocopiable pages 62 and 63

Activity time
I hour

Assessment
▌ Did children use strategies demonstrated to listen to each other's views and preferences?

▌ How effectively were children able to accommodate different views and look for consensus?

Packing for evacuation

Objectives
▌ To listen and respond to each other's ideas

▌ To ask relevant questions of others

▌ To take notes

▌ To negotiate to reach a final decision

You will need
▌ Photocopiable page 64

Activity time
30 minutes

Assessment
▌ Did children listen to others' opinions and ask relevant questions?

▌ Did children use appropriate phrases when negotiating?

Background information
In this activity children are asked to consider the things they would pack in a suitcase when being evacuated and to listen to other's suggestions before negotiating to reach a final decision.

What to do

Divide the class into groups of about four and encourage the children to imagine how parents and children must have felt the night before evacuation. What would people do on this night? Remind the children that television was not an option! Ask the groups to feed back their suggestions to the class. If no one has brought it up, suggest that the evacuees would have packed some of their belongings to take with them on this night. Explain

that a small suitcase was all that was allowed for each evacuee and that some children from poor homes wouldn't even have had this 'luxury'.

Now ask the children to imagine they are evacuees and need to decide what to pack. Provide children with copies of photocopiable page 64 and ask them to look at the list at the top of the page. Why are there no computer games on the list? Why no mobile phones? What other current games/toys were not around in the 1940s? Ask the children to complete the first part of the sheet individually. Remind them that they can add one thing to the list before choosing their top three. You may wish to talk through an example, indicating your reasons why you would pack a particular item. Give children time to do this individually, asking them to make notes in the relevant column about their reasons for choosing their three items. You might want to refresh their memories about writing only the key words and phrases and using abbreviations when making notes.

Next, ask the children to talk about their choices in their groups of four. Remind them to listen carefully to others' reasons and to take notes of these reasons, recording these in the table on the second half of photocopiable page 64. Although children will necessarily be taking turns here, it is important that this does not deteriorate into simply reading notes aloud. Encourage them to ask each other questions to clarify their reasons. For example, if a child said they would take their favourite book, others might ask what the title of this book is, when they first read it, whether it has illustrations and so on. To encourage children to ask questions, you might want to place counters in the middle of each group's table. When a child asks a question of another, they can take a counter. This is a device, if not overused, that can be effective in encouraging children to contribute.

When the children have finished discussing their individual reasons, their next task is to come to a group decision about the three things they would pack. Stop children before they move on to this and explain that you want to hear people showing that they have listened well by referring to other people's reasons and changing their minds. On the board, write phrases like:
- *After hearing Sunita's reason, I think I agree with her now.*
- *Billy's reason sounded really good so now I think we should include...*
- *I like what Anna said about the ___, so now I think...*
- *I hadn't thought of that reason for packing a ___.*
- *Lisa's idea about taking the ___ is great and now I agree with her.*
- *That's a good idea, but...*

and tell children that you will be listening out for these in their discussions.

When all groups have decided on three items, lead a class feedback session to draw out the similarities and differences in choices. Encourage the children to use their notes to justify their decisions. You may want to share your own choices at this point and justify your decisions by agreeing or disagreeing with the children's reasons.

Simplifying the activity
■ After the individual part of the activity, undertake the rest as a class discussion.

Extending the activity
■ Some children could illustrate an open suitcase with the chosen objects inside.
■ Children could adapt the activity to undertake a survey of teachers and/or parents, or children in another class, and compare these choices with their own.

An evacuee's letter home

Objectives
▌ To choose appropriate syntax and vocabulary

▌ To negotiate within groups to reach a joint decision

▌ To use character and narrative to convey ideas

You will need
▌ Photocopiable page 65

▌ Large cardboard thought bubbles and marker pens

Activity time
1 hour

Assessment
▌ Did children avoid the use of modern day words/phrases and therefore use appropriate vocabulary and syntax?

▌ How effective were children's negotiations in reaching a joint decision?

Background information
This activity focuses on letters home during evacuation and helps children to explore characters. Do people always tell the truth in letters? Can letters give clues as to how the writer really feels? The activity also helps children to compare modern and 1940s vocabulary and syntax.

What to do
Revise the fact that children from large towns and cities were evacuated to the countryside during the war and that this often caused more anguish than it was meant to prevent! Discuss how eagerly parents and children must have awaited news from each other and how difficult it must have been to sound cheerful while at the same time letting your

family know that you missed them. Tell the children that they will now be looking at two examples of letters from an evacuee who is missing her mum dreadfully. Issue photocopiable page 65 and discuss as a class the major differences between the two letters and how very often people hide their true feelings in letters so as not to worry those they love. Draw children's attention to times when we might also do this when speaking with, or to, different audiences. Decide as a class which letter Jane should send and why. Draw the children's attention to some of the language features, such as the lack of modern-day phrases. For example, Jane signs her letter *Your loving daughter.* What modern phrase would the children use in a letter home? (Perhaps *Love from…*)

Now tell the children they are going to compose thought bubbles for Jane which depict her true feelings. Explain that eventually these 'thoughts' will be held up above a tableau that the children create of Jane writing the cheerful letter home. Encourage the children to use appropriate language, that is, no modern-day phrases. Organise the children into groups of four or so, and give them particular aspects of Jane's new life to address in their thought bubbles. Ask two groups to focus on the aspect 'Food', two groups to focus on 'Farm animals', another two to focus on 'Travelling to school', and two groups to focus on 'Making friends'. Tell the children that each thought should be no more than ten words.

Each pair of groups should then come together to share their ideas and to negotiate the final version for their thought bubble. Tell the children to be prepared to incorporate others' ideas. Tell them that you will be listening for phrases like, *Your idea sounds better than ours. Let's use this group's idea about... The word you two have used sounds terrific – let's use it instead of the one we had. How about using their good idea about... That sounds interesting.* It might be best to sit with a group that are having difficulty negotiating in order to model the use of such language. Issue each group with a cardboard thought bubble for children to write in their final version.

Children will now need time to rehearse the tableau. In this tableau, one child should depict Jane writing her letter home. As she writes, another child speaks the words of the cheerful letter. Encourage this child to speak slowly, clearly and audibly. At the appropriate points, other children enter carrying the thought bubbles which indicate Jane's true feelings. Each one is held over Jane's head in turn.

Simplifying the activity

■ Omit the tableau. Have a class discussion about which sentences/ phrases/individual words they would choose from each letter home to give a more realistic view of Jane's feelings.

Extending the activity

■ Issue children with highlighter pens and ask them to individually mark the sentences/phrases/ individual words they would choose to write in a letter home. In their groups, they should defend their choices, listen to others and eventually compose a new letter home.

Allocating evacuees

The evacuees

Name		
Age		
Home		
Likes		
Worries		
School progress		
Other information		

A suitable family

	Advantages	Disadvantages
Ashcroft		
Ross		
Hamilton		
Illingworth		

Families for evacuees

The Ashcroft family

The Ashcrofts live in a two-bedroomed terraced house in a small town. Mr Ashcroft works in a munitions factory. He is a good-natured man, but does like peace and quiet. Mrs Ashcroft is a full-time housewife and mother. Their son Billy is 12 and has just started secondary school. He is interested in anything to do with the war and football. He gets on well with his brother Sam, who is 8. Sam occasionally gets into trouble, but is not really a bad boy. There is a small garden at the back. This is the only place the children play, as there are few facilities in the area.

The Ross family

The Ross family live in a small seaside village. The family consists of Granny Ross, her daughter Mrs Ross, two-year-old twins and a young baby. Mr Ross is in France fighting for his country. Granny can't help out as much as she would like to. She enjoys reading and listening to the wireless. Mrs Ross is very busy with her young family. They live in a small old cottage near the harbour. Anyone staying there would need to share a room with the twins.

The Hamiltons

Kathleen Hamilton lives with her mother and father on a dairy farm. She is 14 and is used to being on her own, as her mother and father are busy on the farm. As well as being keen to do well with her schoolwork, Kathleen likes to go for long walks in the woods near the farm and is an expert on local bird life. Mr and Mrs Hamilton are keen for Kathleen to mix more with other children, but Kathleen does not like the idea of sharing her mother and father with evacuees. Anyone coming to live on the farm would be expected to help to look after the animals.

The Illingworths

Mr Illingworth is a doctor. He lives in the country, with his wife Geraldine. They have no children. Mrs Illingworth is a nutritionist who works from home for the Ministry of Food. Both are have little free time. However, they feel they should contribute to the war effort by taking in evacuees as they have a large house and garden. The house is always spotless and the garden is very well looked after, with flowerbeds and vegetable plots. They are nice people, but are not used to looking after children on a daily basis.

Packing for evacuation

▮ Choose three of the following things you would pack when being evacuated.

▪favourite cuddly toy ▪favourite book ▪comic ▪best clothes ▪jigsaw/board game ▪framed photo of your family ▪sweets, paper and pencils ▪torch ▪other: _____

My choices	My reasons

▮ Now listen to other people's reasons for choosing their things.

Things to pack	Notes
favourite cuddly toy	
favourite book	
comic	
best clothes	
jigsaw/board game	
framed photo of your family	
sweets, paper and pencils	
torch	

Our group's final decision:

1. _____   2. _____   3. _____

An evacuee's letter home

Dear Mum

Letter 1

I am missing you lots. When I think of you I am very sad and sometimes I feel like crying at night. I know I am lucky to be safe here in the country and that I should be grateful for the good food to eat now but I would swap all of that for just one slice of bread and dripping shared with you.

Every day we walk half a mile to the school and half a mile back. The school has only one classroom. There are only two children in the class who talk to me.

We have to pass lots of fields on the way to school and some of them have real bulls in them. I get scared. Hens run about the farm and they try to peck me. I call the big red one Nicky.

Please write soon and send me a photo of you to cheer me up.

Your loving daughter, Jane

XXXXX

Letter 2

Dear Mum

You would love this farm! The food here is different from ours at home and we can have eggs whenever we want. Sometimes I am allowed to collect them from the hen house. At first I was a little frightened of the hens but now I know them all and they know me. I have even given names to some of them!

When I walk to school with all the other children we sing funny songs about Hitler and we have started to make up other verses. I have made two new friends called Maggie and Liz.

Do write soon, please!

Your loving daughter, Jane

XXXXX

SCHOLASTIC

Interviewing an evacuee

Did anyone from your family come and visit you?

Where were you evacuated to?

What was the thing you missed most about home?

What were the people like that you stayed with?

How did you keep in touch with your family?

How long were you evacuated for?

Would you ever send your own children away?

What things did you take with you when you were evacuated?

What was the best thing about being away from home?

Were any of your family sent to the same place?

How did you get to the place you were evacuated to?

What did/didn't you like about living in the country?

Photocopiable

Village settlers

Linked to
The National Curriculum
for geography, Key Stage 2,
'Knowledge and understanding
of places';
Scottish environmental studies
5–14 guidelines, social subjects,
'People and place'

Activity	speaking	listening	group discussion	drama
1. Ordnance survey symbols photocopiable pages 75 and 76		▌respond to others	▌make relevant contributions ▌qualify or justify ▌deal politely with opposing views	
2. The village for us photocopiable pages 77 and 78		▌ask relevant questions ▌respond to others	▌make relevant contributions ▌qualify or justify ▌deal politely with opposing views	
3. Choosing a place to live photocopiable page 79		▌respond to others	▌make relevant contributions ▌deal politely with opposing views ▌help the group to move forward	
4. Naming villages photocopiable pages 80 and 81	▌show shape and organisation ▌speak audibly and clearly ▌choose material that is relevant ▌gain and maintain the response of different audiences		▌qualify or justify	

Ordnance survey symbols

Objectives
▌ To explore alternatives and reach agreement

▌ To follow up on others' points

You will need
▌ Photocopiable pages 75 and 76

Activity time
1 hour

Assessment
▌ Did children explore alternatives?

▌ How successfully did they reach agreement?

▌ Were children able to follow up on each other's points?

Background information
Particular landscape features have been selected for this activity. It would be interesting for the children if these are supplemented with photographs and symbols of features specific to their own environment.

What to do
First, develop the children's understanding of what a *symbol* is, perhaps by referring to ones with which they may already be familiar, such as male/female toilet symbols, disabled symbols, danger symbols and so on. Some key points to establish are that:
▬ symbol should be a clear, simple image related to the object or concept that it is representing
▬ the image has to be easily recognised by as many people as possible
▬ the image usually represents without the support of words.

Next, put the children into pairs and issue each pair with photocopiable page 75 and some additional paper for experimenting with designs. Tell the children that they are going to work together to design symbols for each of the pictures on the sheet. Demonstrate, with another child as your partner, modelling how they might explore alternatives and reach agreement. Use a feature not included on the photocopiable page, such as a campsite. Useful language might include, *Some tents are triangle shaped, but others aren't. What shape do you think we should use? We could put on the ropes to hold the tent down. Should we include lots of that shape to show that it isn't just one tent? I think we should only put one tent, but I like your idea about the ropes.*

Once pairs have designed their own symbols, issue the Ordnance Survey symbols, cut into cards, from photocopiable page 76. Explain briefly the purpose of Ordnance Survey symbols (the need for standardised versions of symbols on maps; the need for something that doesn't take up much room, is easily recognisable and so on). Ask the children to match the symbols on the cards they have been given with the pictures on photocopiable page 75. Explain that they have more symbols than pictures and to keep the ones that don't match up to one side for now.

Remind the children about the points outlined previously in relation to an effective symbol. Bearing these in mind, ask the children to discuss which symbol for each feature they think is more effective – the Ordnance Survey version or their own. Before they do this, model ways of following up on others' points, for example, *I agree with what you are saying about ___ , but I think... So you think that... because... I think you are right because... I don't agree with... as...* Explain that you will be listening out for children using these phrases. Ask each pair to choose two features: one where they think their symbol is more effective and one where they think the Ordnance Survey symbol is more effective. Direct them to write out the two sentences below based on their choices.

▪ We think our symbol for ___ is better than the Ordnance Survey symbol because...

▪ We think the Ordnance Survey symbol for ___ is better than ours because...

Join each pair up with another pair and ask them to explain their conclusions to each other.

Regroup the children into their original pairs and direct them to the Ordnance Survey symbols they have been given for *electricity line, footpath* and *picnic site*. Ask them to experiment with ways of modifying these symbols to give them a greater impact. Display and compare the children's ideas.

Simplifying the activity

▪ Do not ask children to work with the three additional symbols on photocopiable page 76.

Extending the activity

▪ Encourage the children to collect other Ordnance Survey symbols and make these into an information leaflet for parents or other children.

▪ Ask the children to use the symbols to create a desirable settlement and simple key.

▪ Ask the children to find the symbols on an Ordnance Survey map. With children in groups, this could be a game.

The village for us

Objectives
▌ To accommodate different preferences

▌ To provide and gather information through asking and answering relevant questions

You will need
▌ Photocopiables pages 77 and 78

▌ Basic Ordnance Survey symbols for reference – available on www.ordsvy.gov.uk

Activity time
1 hour

Assessment
▌ How did children accommodate different preferences?

▌ Were children able to provide and gather information through asking and answering relevant questions?

Background information
Rather than children gathering information about different villages through reading and writing alone, the information exchange phase of the activity provides children with a focused and tightly structured means of obtaining information through speaking and listening.

The village maps provided for this activity are taken from different parts of the UK. An alternative would be to use maps of villages close to the children's environment. The website www.villagesonline.com will provide you and the children with maps and additional information about local villages. The selection of symbols for children to choose from is based on features arising in the maps provided. This selection could be modified if maps of more local villages are used.

What to do
Organise the class into pairs and issue them with photocopiable page 77. Direct the children to the symbols at the top of the sheet and ask each pair to decide on five features they would like their imaginary village to have. Encourage the children to think about the implications of choosing particular features. For example, if they choose a campsite and a caravan site they are likely to have a lot of holidaymakers. This might be regarded as desirable or undesirable. Because individual preferences will differ, it would be useful to model how the children might accommodate these, for example *I would like to have a ___ in the village because…. Do you think that would be a good idea? I think it would be nice to have a ___, but I don't think it is as important/useful as… So we agree on three features. Maybe we should try to find another one that we both like. I think this one might be better than that one because… What*

do you think? When the children have agreed on their five features, tell them to draw the symbols in the left-hand column of the table on the bottom half of the photocopiable sheet.

Now issue each pair with one of the maps from photocopiable page 78 (enlarged). Ask them to examine the map of the village area they have been given for any features they have chosen. Tell them to tick these features off on the table on photocopiable page 77. Demonstrate to the class how they should do this. Ask the children to note other features the village has in the space provided, paying particular attention to the features/symbols listed at the top of the sheet. Make sets of Ordnance Survey symbols available for reference at this point.

Allow about 15 minutes for each pair to note the features of the village based on the map they were given.

Once they have done this, organise the class into groups of four, one child from each of four pairs, in such a way that each child has information about a different village. Show the children how to share the information they have gathered about the different villages. This would include modelling how to ask relevant questions, for example, *Did any of the villages have a railway?* and how to frame responses, *Yes, Xxxx has a railway*. Guidance should also be offered about taking turns to ask and answer questions and giving everyone in the group time to interpret their table and note responses.

When the information exchange has been completed (about 20 minutes), return children to their original pairs. Ask them to decide which village is nearest to their requirements, based on the information they have gathered. Then pull the class together and establish which villages met the most requirements.

Simplifying the activity

■ Organise the class into groups of eight in such a way that each of the four pairs has information about a different village. In this way the responsibility for asking questions, noting information and offering information is shared.

Extending the activity

■ Direct children to www.villagesonline.com to find a village with more of the features they have selected. There are Ordnance Survey maps for some of the villages to help children with this.

■ Ask children also to select a feature that they do *not* want in their village, and be able to tell you why.

Naming villages

Objectives
▪ To give a short presentation to an audience

▪ To keep the interest of audience members by scanning and involving them in some way

▪ To justify reasons for choices

You will need
▪ Some information on local place names from a local library or the Internet

▪ Photocopiable page 80 – one copy for each group of four children

▪ The word parts from photocopiable page 80 enlarged and made into individual cards

▪ Photocopiable page 81

Activity time
1 hour

Assessment
▪ Did children scan the audience and attempt to involve them in any way?

▪ Were children's voices audible?

Background information
This activity should follow the other activities in which children have had the opportunity to examine features of locations. The task is based on the examination of current place names and has been devised to help children consider how place names have come about. The children are asked to invent names for given places and will deliver a presentation on their name choice to the class.

What to do
Revise the main geographical features of early settlements and refer children to their previous work on locations. It might be best to discuss their own location's name at this point and to use photocopiable page 80 (or other reference material) to try to decode the meaning of their locality's name. Ask them to look at the location they chose in the previous activity and tell them that they are now going to think of a good name for this place.

Divide the class into groups of four (the children in each group having chosen the same location in the previous activity) and issue each group with photocopiable page 80. Ask them to read the definitions and tick the name parts that relate to the features of their location. Then, issue cards cut out from photocopiable page 80 and ask the children to pick out the cards appropriate to their location. This will enable them to play about with the order of the parts of words so that the eventual name sounds and looks to their liking.

Children should now get ready to present their names and the explanations to the class. The planning sheet on photocopiable page 81 might guide groups with this and also help them to allocate parts of the presentation to all members in the group. Tell the children that you will be looking for presenters to scan the audience, speak audibly and encourage the audience to ask questions or to undertake a small task, such as decoding another name for a village. Allow children time to rehearse their presentations and perhaps to present to another group before going in front of a larger audience.

Simplifying the activity
▪ You may want to model scanning an audience (ensuring that you look *regularly* at all sections of the audience) and speaking audibly by giving a short mock presentation on the name of a village.
▪ You may also want to list ideas for involving the audience, for example inviting questions, asking them to decode given names, asking them to devise a name for a village with given features.

Extending the activity
▪ Challenge the children to devise a quiz for others (other groups, other classes, parents, teachers) to decode names of villages.
▪ Ask children to present to a larger audience.

Designing symbols

Our symbols

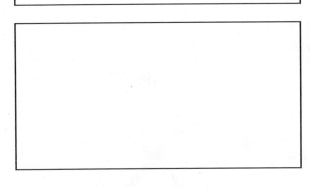

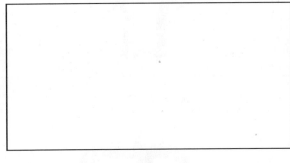

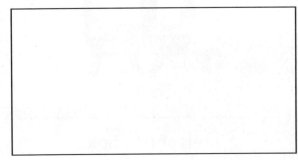

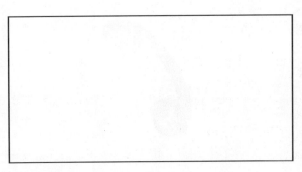

Matching symbols

railway track	electricity line
————————	⋏ ⋏ ⋏

windmill	church with spire

caravan site	footpath
	· ·

telephone box	picnic site

Photocopiable

The village for us

▮ Choose five features you would like your village to have.

▮ Draw the symbols you have chosen in the first column of the table below.

▮ Examine the map you have been given. If this village has any of the features that you want, tick them in the table. Note other interesting features the village has in the space provided.

▮ Now take turns to ask and answer questions in your group to gather information about all four villages.

Features/ symbols	Villages			
	Gargrave	Comrie	Hyde Heath	Llancarfan
Other features				

▮ The village most similar to the one we would like to live in is

_____

Village maps

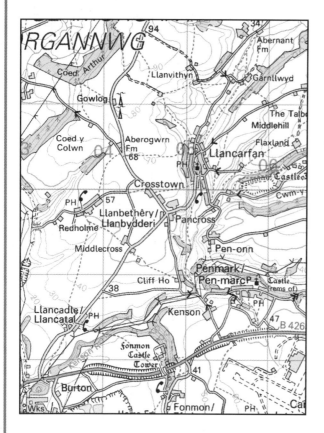

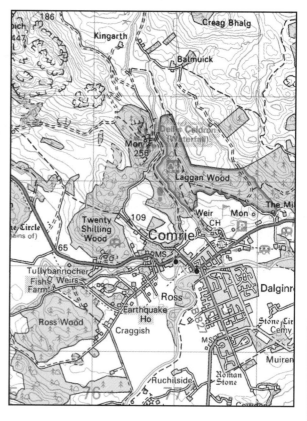

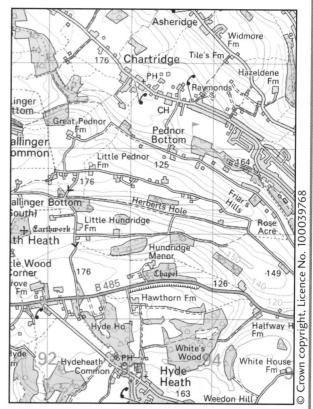

Choosing a place to live

Location A	This would mean…	Location B	This would mean…
deep, fast-flowing river		river that sometimes floods the land	
no safe place to cross the river		river has good places to cross it	
forest nearby		forest on hills about 1km away	
stony grassland		flat grassland with very few stones	
soil is excellent		soil is quite good	

We think that we would settle in Location _____ because _____

_____

_____

The feature we would most like to add to our place is _____

_____

because _____

_____

SCHOLASTIC

Linked to
The National Curriculum for history, Key Stage 2, 'A world history study';
Scottish environmental studies 5–14 guidelines, social subjects, 'People in the past'

The Egyptians

Activity	speaking	listening	group discussion	drama
1. Antique roadshow photocopiable pages 88 and 89		▌respond to others	▌make relevant contributions ▌deal politely with opposing views ▌explore ideas and evaluate contributions	
2. Presenting an Egyptian artefact	▌speak audibly and clearly ▌gain and maintain the response of different audiences	▌recall and re-present important features	▌make relevant contributions ▌take up and sustain different roles ▌explore ideas and evaluate contributions	▌evaluate contributions ▌create, adapt and sustain different roles
3. Tutankhamun photocopiable page 90		▌ask relevant questions ▌recall and re-present important features		
4. Interesting facts	▌show shape and organisation ▌speak audibly and clearly ▌choose material that is relevant ▌use appropriate vocabulary and syntax	▌respond to others ▌identify gist/ key points		▌explore characters and issues

Antique roadshow

Background information
This activity gives the children the opportunity to observe pictures of Egyptian artefacts and to decide in their groups what each artefact was used for and whom the artefact might have belonged to.

What to do

Ask the children what they already know about Ancient Egypt. Record their ideas on the board. As you record them, try to group them into categories such as 'daily life', 'houses' and 'death'. Highlight where Egypt is located on a map. Discuss the surrounding countries and the river Nile. Explain that the Nile was an important source of water to irrigate the desert and allowed the cultivation of crops that were needed for the growing population. Allow the children to phrase questions that they would like to research or that they may wish to ask other children. Children could be given the opportunity to say what they have read (or have not) previously on the topic, for example, *I am really interested in mummification, would anyone like to ask me a question? I haven't read any books on the Egyptians, could anyone recommend one?*

When the class discussion has come to an end, split the class into pairs. Provide each pair with a picture of an Egyptian artefact from photocopiable page 88 and ask them to discuss what the artefact might have been used for. Issue photocopiable page 89 to help focus their discussion a little more here, explaining that they should answer *True* or *False* for each of the statements about their object. You may wish to go over one of the artefacts as an example with the whole class. *What do you think it is made of? What do you think this artefact was used for? Why do you think that? Do you think it is heavy or light? Does anyone have any different ideas?* Tell the children that you will be listening for them justifying their ideas and using phrases such as, *This thing looks funny and I think I'd like to play with it* or *My mum wouldn't let me touch that. It looks dangerous, so it can't be a toy.*

Each pair should now join with another pair that has been looking at a picture of the same object to make a group of four. Tell each group to compare their true and false statements, and encourage the children to listen to each other's reasons. Ask the group of four to negotiate their true/false conclusions. Advise the children that you will be listening for them to respond politely to differing points of view. You want to hear them use phrases such as, *That was a good idea, but I think… or, I know what you're saying, but if we look closely here we can see…* Allow

Objectives
▌ To respond to others

▌ To justify opinions by drawing upon evidence

▌ To deal politely with opposing views

You will need
▌ Photocopiable pages 88 and 89

▌ Information sources on Egyptian artefacts

Activity time
1 hour 15 minutes

Assessment
▌ Did children respond to each other's ideas?

▌ Did children use modelled phrases to other children in their groups?

the children 15 minutes to discuss their artefact and to record their ideas about what it might be (and reasons why) at the bottom of photocopiable page 89.

Gather the class together and allow each group to say what they think the artefact is and why. Allow time for the children to say how they managed opposing views, for example, *We disagreed at the beginning of the discussion, but Colin then explained very clearly why he thought it was a ___ and we then decided that we liked his idea. In our group we said that it was important to listen to everyone's ideas before we finally decided. Saima and John still don't think it is a ___, so we are going to research to try to discover what it is.*

Explain to the children that they are now going to research using books and/or the Internet to gain further information about their artefact. The group should now split to work in pairs. Two children could research on the web and the other two could research in the

library. Before the pairs do this, you may or may not wish to confirm with them what the artefacts actually are:

Artefact 1: 'dogs and jackals' game (a game board in the shape of a frog with 29 holes – the short sticks made of bone or wood represented the jackals)

Artefact 2: ivory hair comb (Egyptian hair combs often had elaborately carved handles in the form of animals or birds)

Artefact 3: cosmetic palette in the shape of a ram (used to mix or grind eye paints)

Artefact 4: game of 'snake' (the stone board represents a coiled snake with its eye in the centre; players would move counters – stone balls – round the squares towards the middle of the board)

Artefact 5: sacred rattle (used in ceremonies by noblewomen and priestesses; linked to the goddess of music and dance)

Artefact 6: Canopic jar (used to store the internal organs of mummified dead).

Allow 30 minutes for the children to conduct their research. Explain that they will then come together to finalise the information. Check that all groups are working well and that they are evaluating each other's ideas, using phrases such as, *That's a good idea, but what about... I was wondering if... or...* Gather the class together and tell the children to quickly note their ideas for the following lesson.

Simplifying the activity

■ The children could be given clues to help them identify the object.

Extending the activity

■ The children could individually record their ideas in table format before moving to the group situation. They should be encouraged to give clear reasons to justify their thinking.

Presenting an Egyptian artefact

Background information
This activity builds on the previous one and helps children to prepare and undertake a simple presentation about their Egyptian artefact. The purpose of this session is to help children focus very precisely on a limited number of aspects of speaking to an audience. These are reflected in the objectives above. You may decide to change the focus here to suit your class's needs.

What to do
Remind the children of their research and what they have discovered about their artefact. Tell them not to reveal what their artefact is at this point as the class will be hearing all about it in the presentations.

Discuss what makes an effective presentation, for example interaction with audience; logical sequence; visual stimulus; pacing; scanning the audience. Record ideas on the board. Explain that for this presentation they will remain in their groups of four and will be focusing on using a logical sequence, scanning their audience, and speaking at an appropriate pace. The presentation should last approximately four minutes. Ask the children to order their talk in four steps to sequence their presentation. The four steps might be:
- one short introductory sentence which states what each member of the group's duty will be
- giving facts
- giving their opinions, feelings, viewpoints
- one sentence to round off the presentation.

Give the children 20 minutes to prepare their talk. Before they present, it might be best for you to give a mock presentation and ask children to grade you. You could split the class into two groups, each focusing on only one aspect. You could decide to give a poor presentation then listen to advice before attempting an improved version. This would give children an opportunity to articulate their opinions and would create an atmosphere where the teacher shows a willingness to listen to others' advice. Although children may offer advice on many aspects of presentation, let them know that you want good pacing and scanning in particular.

Simplifying the activity
- Groups which need support could work closely with the classroom assistant or the teacher during the planning stages.

Extending the activity
- Groups could devise their own criteria for their presentation.

Objectives
- To scan the audience during a presentation
- To present information in a logical sequence
- To speak at an appropriate pace during a presentation

Activity time
1 hour 20 minutes

Assessment
- Was the content of presentations appropriate and in a logical sequence?
- Were children able to scan and speak simultaneously?

Tutankhamun

Objectives
▌ To respond to others

▌ To make relevant contributions

You will need
▌ Photocopiable page 90

Activity time
1 hour

Assessment
▌ Did children respond to suggestions made by others?

▌ Did children make relevant contributions during the discussion?

Background information
This lesson focuses on Tutankhamun. The children will read a short passage which will then be discussed in groups of four. They will then be expected to come to agreement about how Tutankhmun died.

What to do
Tell the children you are going to talk to them about Tutankhamun. Ask everyone to listen carefully to the passage on photocopiable page 90 as you read it to them. Explore key questions, for example *Can anyone tell me what a pharaoh was? Do you think it would be a difficult task being a king at the age of nine? Why do you think his priests made sure he had a spectacular funeral? Little is known about this famous pharaoh; I wonder what his life was really like. What do you think?* Allow time for the children to ask their own questions and discuss any other points of interest. Explain to the children that historians don't really know how Tutankhamun died.

Tell the children that they will be working in pairs to discuss how they think Tutankhamun might have died. Once they have discussed a variety of ideas, they should select three suggestions before they join another pair for further discussion. The children may wish to note their ideas. Remind them that they will need to discuss how the head injury occurred; if it was an accident or murder. Model phrases the children could use, such as, *I think it must have been an accident as… He was given a spectacular funeral so it must have been an accident. Because he went back to the old religion I think someone might have killed him.* Allow ten minutes for the children to debate and record their ideas.

Ask each pair to join with another pair and come to an agreement on how Tutankhamun died. Model how to listen to each other's ideas and to negotiate, for example, *I think that is a better idea as… We didn't think he had been killed as we thought everyone liked him. We thought that, but… I think I would like to change our idea as we didn't talk about… I would like to suggest that we go with Amy's idea…* Remind the children that they have to decide on one main idea. Allow the children five to ten minutes to discuss their ideas.

Tell the groups that you want them to decide on a newspaper headline related to their ideas. Explore different headlines with the children, for example, *King dies in mysterious circumstances; King falls to a tragic death; Was it an accident?* Display the headlines created.

Simplifying the activity
▨ Remove the requirement to create a headline.

Extending the activity
▨ Children could present a talk on how they think Tutankhamun died.

Interesting facts

Background information
This activity involves children researching the lives of famous Ancient Egyptians. This activity might best be undertaken near the end of the topic.

What to do
Explain to the children that they are going to be researching four famous Ancient Egyptians, for example King Akhenaten, Anubis the first Embalmer, Nefertiti (wife of Akhenaten) and Ramesses II. You may decide to change the people to be researched in relation to the focus of the topic your class has been working on. Organise the children into groups of four and allocate each child a person to research. Write some possible headings on the board into order to focus the children's research, for example *Main achievement, Main failing, Official reason for death*. Encourage the children to use a variety of resources to research their information.

When the children have researched for about 20 minutes, ask them to return to their groups. Tell them that they are going to use the information they have gathered to be in a hot-seat, answering questions from the rest of the group, in role as the person allocated.

Model key questions that the children may wish to ask, such as, *Who are you? Why were you important? How did you die?* Encourage the child in role to add expression and facial responses and to consider if the person would be serious or flippant. Encourage the other children to take turns in asking questions and to organise the order independently, with little intervention from you. The children may wish to ask further questions and should be encouraged to do so. Your role here should be to observe from a distance to allow the children to participate fully in role. After each child has had a turn of hot-seating, gather the children together. Discuss key facts discovered and ask the children to tell you what they liked/disliked about hot-seating. What did they learn from it?

Simplifying the activity
■ Put the children into pairs to research the person selected.
■ Select simplified texts or collate main points for the children.

Extending the activity
■ Encourage children to prepare additional questions.
■ After the interviewing session, children could prepare a three-minute presentation about their chosen Ancient Egyptian.

Objectives
■ To speak audibly and clearly
■ To ask relevant questions

You will need
■ Information texts about the Egyptians

Activity time
1 hour

Assessment
■ Did children ask relevant questions?
■ Did children speak clearly during their hot-seating interview?

Tutankhamun

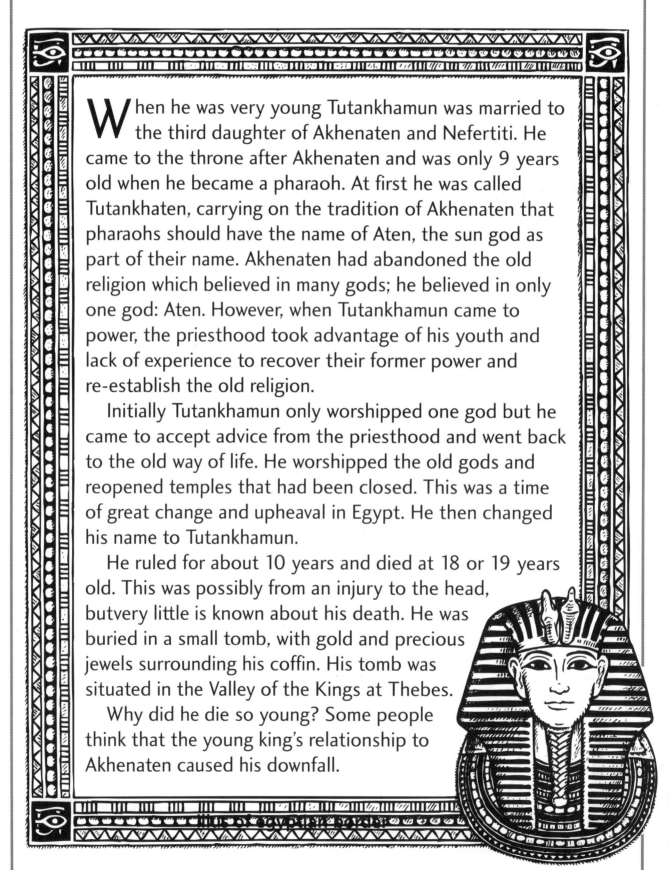

When he was very young Tutankhamun was married to the third daughter of Akhenaten and Nefertiti. He came to the throne after Akhenaten and was only 9 years old when he became a pharaoh. At first he was called Tutankhaten, carrying on the tradition of Akhenaten that pharaohs should have the name of Aten, the sun god as part of their name. Akhenaten had abandoned the old religion which believed in many gods; he believed in only one god: Aten. However, when Tutankhamun came to power, the priesthood took advantage of his youth and lack of experience to recover their former power and re-establish the old religion.

Initially Tutankhamun only worshipped one god but he came to accept advice from the priesthood and went back to the old way of life. He worshipped the old gods and reopened temples that had been closed. This was a time of great change and upheaval in Egypt. He then changed his name to Tutankhamun.

He ruled for about 10 years and died at 18 or 19 years old. This was possibly from an injury to the head, butvery little is known about his death. He was buried in a small tomb, with gold and precious jewels surrounding his coffin. His tomb was situated in the Valley of the Kings at Thebes.

Why did he die so young? Some people think that the young king's relationship to Akhenaten caused his downfall.

The Vikings

Linked to
The National Curriculum for history, Key Stage 2, 'Vikings in Britain';
Scottish environmental studies 5–14 guidelines, social subjects, 'People in the past'

Activity	speaking	listening	group discussion	drama
1. What would you ask a Viking? photocopiable page 100		▌respond to others	▌make relevant contributions ▌qualify or justify ▌deal politely with opposing views ▌help the group to move forward	
2. Researching the answers photocopiable page 101	▌speak audibly and clearly	▌identify features of language used for a specific purpose ▌recall and re-present important features ▌respond to others	▌make relevant contributions ▌qualify or justify ▌explore ideas and evaluate contributions ▌help the group to move forward	
3. Interview with a Viking	▌choose material that is relevant ▌evaluate speech ▌gain and maintain the response of different audiences	▌ask relevant questions ▌identify features of language used for a specific purpose ▌respond to others		▌explore characters and issues ▌evaluate contributions ▌create, adapt and sustain different roles
4. To settle or move on?		▌recall and re-present important features ▌respond to others ▌identify gist/key points	▌make relevant contributions ▌qualify or justify ▌deal politely with opposing views	▌explore characters and issues ▌create, adapt and sustain different roles ▌use character, action and narrative to convey ideas

What would you ask a Viking?

Objectives
▌ To put forward ideas and justify them

▌ To listen to the ideas of others and evaluate them

▌ To reach a consensus in a group

You will need
▌ photocopiable page 100

Activity time
1 hour

Assessment
▌ Did children put forward their own ideas and justify them?

▌ Did they listen to and evaluate the ideas of others?

▌ Did they reach a group consensus?

Background information
This activity and the rest in this unit would be useful when the class are working on a Viking case study in history. The children will be expected to have some knowledge of the Vikings to bring to these speaking and listening activities. Access to books on the Vikings will be necessary for research. This first activity involves the children talking in groups to decide on questions to ask a Viking in an interview (see 'Interview with a Viking', page 96).

What to do
Introduce the activity by asking the children, *If you met a Viking what would you like to ask him or her?* Record the children's suggestions on the board. They might suggest:

▩ What is your name?

▩ Where do you live?

▩ Do you have a longboat?

▩ Do you wear a helmet?

▩ Why did you come to Britain?

Explain to the children that there are probably lots of questions we would like to ask. Tell them that later they are going to interview a Viking (a child in role).

At this point, explore with the children what they know about interviews and interviewing. Have they seen people interviewing or being interviewed on television? Elicit from them that, generally, there is one person asking questions – the interviewer – and one person answering the questions – the interviewee. Tell the children to put themselves in the position of the interviewer. How do they think an interviewer prepares for an interview? Explain that interviewers don't just ask any old questions that come into their heads; they prepare most of the questions in advance. Explore why this would be important, for example:

▮ Questions need to be relevant – you would not ask a Viking about the Victorians or about how to make an electric circuit.

▮ Questions need to be focused – you would not ask, *What's it like to be a Viking?* because this is too general and the answer would be vague. It would be better to ask, *Are you a settler or an invader?* because this has a clear focus.

▮ Questions need to be organised in a logical order. It would not be sensible or easy to follow if the questions jumped about from how Vikings travelled to what they ate, to where they settled, to what they wore.

It might be useful to display these three key interview points on a poster.

Put the children into groups of about four (aiming to have eight groups altogether). Explain that they are going to decide on questions to ask a Viking and consider how to organise the questions. This will ensure the interview covers all the important questions and is done in an order that makes the interview flow. Introduce photocopiable page 100 and allocate one of Viking boy, girl, man or woman to each group to prepare questions for.

The first task for the group is to read each question in turn, think about it individually, decide for themselves if it is a relevant and suitable question, be able to say why, then discuss in the group whether to choose this question or not. Model this with an example – *We are going to be interviewing a Viking boy. Would 'Do you go to school?' be a suitable question? Fiona says, 'Yes, it would be a good question to ask a Viking boy because it is important to find out if they went to school or not.'*

Remind the children that they must listen to everyone's ideas before coming to a decision. If they cannot agree they should try to persuade others or be willing to change their mind, or take a majority decision. Once they have decided they should highlight the chosen questions on the photocopiable sheet.

The groups now need to note which heading their chosen questions would come under: *Personal, Work or school* or *Travel.* Suggest that these will be good headings to use when they are organising their questions.

When the groups have done this, explain that they now have to select three questions under each heading to be used in the interview. To do this, the group will go through a similar process as before: selecting individually and being able to explain their choice of questions under each heading; discussing this as a group and coming to a decision on which questions to choose. When the three questions have been decided on for

each heading these should be recorded on a separate piece of paper. They will need this interview sheet for the next activity.

Simplifying the activity
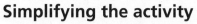 The questions on photocopiable page 100 could be organised in advance into the three headings. Some groups may also need support with reading the questions.

Extending the activity
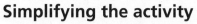 More able children could generate their own questions and would not need photocopiable page 100.

Researching the answers

Objectives
▌ To put forward their ideas clearly

▌ To share information, explaining clearly what they have researched

▌ To come to a group decision

You will need
▌ Interview sheets from the previous activity

▌ Reference books on the Vikings

▌ Access to the Internet (optional)

▌ Photocopiable page 101

Activity time
1 hour 30 minutes

Assessment
▌ Did children put forward their ideas clearly?

▌ Did children share information, explaining clearly what they have researched?

▌ Did children talk together to come to a group decision?

Background information
This activity uses the interview questions prepared in the previous activity. It allows each group to research and decide on possible answers. It would be useful to pair groups to allow each group to research another group's questions. For example:
Groups A and B made up the interview questions to ask a Viking girl.
Groups C and D made up the interview questions to ask a Viking man.
Group A should now take Group C's questions to research, and vice versa.
Group B should take Group D's questions, and vice versa.
Groups E and F made up the interview questions to ask a Viking boy.
Groups G and H made up the interview questions to ask a Viking woman.
Group E should now take Group G's questions to research, and vice versa.
Group F should take Group H's questions, and vice versa.

What to do
Remind the children of the previous activity where they produced the interview sheets. Explain that it is common practice for interviewees to see the questions in advance of the interview in order to prepare for it. This is what the children will be working on today.

The first task is for one person in each group to read out the nine questions under the three headings on the interview sheet. Model with one or two questions in a clear voice.

Explain that some questions will need to be researched. Others can be discussed immediately. The immediate ones would include personal questions on names, age, family size and composition and where the person lives. The groups should look at the information on photocopiable page 101 to help them to come to decisions on these types of questions. Model how to approach this: *What if you read a question that asked, 'What is your name?'? How would your group decide? Let's look at the list of names on this sheet.* Read out the names for males or females. *Which name would you choose? Aftab says he likes Olaf because it is short and there was a king called Olaf who was brave. Sonia likes Harald because it is like Harold and you could call him Harry.* Encourage the children to make suggestions and give reasons. The same procedure could be modelled for surnames and place names. The children may want to locate the place names on a map before they decide.

Remind the children that it is important for everyone in the group to contribute, for everyone to listen politely and for the group to agree. If there is disagreement or a decision is difficult to come to, remind the children that they should:
▨ try to persuade each other through discussion
▨ be willing to change their minds
▨ go with the majority by voting if they have to.

Set the groups 15 minutes to answer the personal questions and allocate one person as scribe to record the answers.

Explain the next task to the groups. They still have to find answers to the questions under the headings *Work or school* and *Travel*. Encourage them to read the questions and consider where they will find the answers to these. They will probably suggest reference books or the Internet. Explain that they are now going to work in pairs to research answers. While they are researching, explain that they should take notes and only focus on answers to their questions. Set the pairs 15 minutes to research their questions and return with their notes to the group.

When they return to the group, each pair should report their findings on each answer. Emphasise the need to report back in a clear voice, keep the report to the point and answer the questions. Model this by answering some of the questions in a quiet, muffled voice or by wandering off the point or not answering the question. Ask the children if they can identify what is wrong and how it should be improved. Model again in a positive way, making the key points clear to the children.

The children should now report their research and the scribe should record their answers to the questions. The groups are now ready to be interviewed.

Simplifying the activity

■ You could prepare an information sheet on the Vikings for the children to use for their research. This could be limiting but may help some to focus.

Extending the activity

■ More able children might like the opportunity to be more independent and could work through the tasks without interruption.

Interview with a Viking

Objectives
▌ To speak audibly, clearly and with appropriate expression

▌ To ask or answer questions and show audience awareness

▌ To listen in order to respond

▌ To take on and sustain a role

You will need
▌ One mock microphone per group (optional)

▌ One clapperboard per group (optional)

▌ A colleague to carry out an interview with you

Activity time
1 hour

Assessment
▌ Did children speak audibly, clearly and with appropriate expression?

▌ Did children ask or answer questions and show audience awareness?

▌ Did children listen, and respond appropriately?

▌ Did children sustain roles?

Background information
All groups should now have prepared questions and prepared answers. Each group is paired with another group. In this activity the children will work in their groups, with one person in the group taking the role of interviewer and one person in the paired group taking on the role of interviewee. They will swap roles during the activity.

What to do
Explain to the class that they are now ready to interview a Viking. Remind them of how an interview is conducted by exploring their knowledge from television interviews. The key points to make will be:

▌ Interviews usually involve two people – the interviewer who asks the questions and the interviewee who will answer them.

▌ The interviewer usually welcomes the interviewee before asking questions.

▌ The interviewee usually says they are *very glad to be here*.

▌ The interviewer may have notes or questions to refer to.

▌ The interviewee does not have notes.

▌ The interviewer will try to follow up the answer given rather than just moving on to the next question.

▌ Both interviewer and interviewee speak clearly with appropriate intonation and at a reasonable speed; make good eye contact and use appropriate body language as a good listener.

■ Each listens closely to the other in order to respond.

It would be useful to record these key points on the board.

The best way to exemplify this would be to ask a colleague to work with you. You could take on the role of a Viking and your colleague could be the interviewer. The first few questions could be modelled badly and the children could be asked to bring out the bad points by using the statements on the board. Encourage them to criticise and evaluate by posing questions, such as:

■ Did I make good eye contact?

■ Did Ms B ask suitable questions?

■ Did we both speak clearly? Could you hear the questions and answers?

■ Did Ms B listen to my answers and try to follow up on them? Can you give an example of this?

This could be followed by modelling some questions and answers correctly and exploring the good points.

Organise the children into their paired groups – A and C, B and D, E and G, F and H. Explain to the children that they are now going to act out the interviews. Only two people will be involved directly in the interview, but all will get a turn as interviewee or interviewer. When they are not involved they should watch the others and give them feedback afterwards, just as they did after watching the teachers.

The children should now be able to take on their roles. Give them some time to re-read the questions or answers to become familiar with them. This will also help them to get into role. Give each pair five minutes to act out the interview and allow two to five minutes feedback before moving on to the next pair. Ensure that both sets of questions and answers are used. Use your own time effectively to monitor, observe, support and give feedback on good points and ways to improve.

The children may want to introduce a clapperboard for *Take 1* and so on, and to use a mock microphone.

They may wish to select the best interviews to show to the rest of the class, another class, the head teacher or parents.

Simplifying the activity

■ This could be carried out as a class activity with the children conducting the interviews in pairs.

■ Less confident groups may need support to remain in role. This could be helped by the presence of an adult with the group.

Extending the activity

■ The activity could be extended by having a panel of interviewers questioning a panel of Vikings. The children would then have to select the appropriate questions for the Viking they wished to address. This would also make listening and responding more challenging.

To settle or move on?

Objectives

▌ To brainstorm ideas in a group

▌ To take on and sustain role

▌ To use character and narrative to convey ideas

Activity time
1 hour

Assessment

▌ Did children brainstorm ideas in a group?

▌ Did children take on and sustain role?

▌ Did children use character and narrative to convey ideas?

Background information
This activity can stand alone within a history focus or as a speaking and listening activity at any point in the sequence of activities in this unit.

What to do

Explain to the children that today they are going to become people in Viking times. They may be a Viking family trying to decide whether to remain in Britain or to travel again and settle elsewhere *or* they may be villagers either persuading the Viking family to stay or encouraging them to continue to travel. There will be arguments on both sides. Rehearse some of these with the children. Why should the family stay? Do the children have any ideas? They may suggest because the family have friends and family here; they have land and a house; it is dangerous to travel. Why should they leave? Travel is exciting; they could see interesting places and make new friends; they could get rich.

Explain to the children that they are going to work in their groups (three or four of each) on either *reasons to settle* or *reasons to move on*. Ask the groups to brainstorm their ideas, and one person in each group – the scribe – should record all the ideas. Bring the groups back together after ten minutes. Display the brainstorms and ask one person from each group to read out their ideas. Explore the 'settle' arguments first and then the 'move on' arguments.

Explain to the children that it is now time for the Viking family to listen to some advice and decide whether they should stay or move on. Select one group to be the Viking family. Ask the group to decide between them who will be adults (for example farmers) and who will be children. Split the rest of the class into two groups – those who will rehearse arguments for staying and those who will rehearse arguments for moving on. Encourage the Viking family to remain in role throughout the activity.

Explain to the other children that they are going to make a 'conscience alley'. On one side of the alley, lined up, are those who have been working on reasons to stay and settle. Lined up on the other side of the alley are those who have been working on reasons to keep travelling. The family members have to move through the alley between the two lines. As they do so, the children on both should whisper reasons to either stay or continue travelling.

If the class has not done this before, the children on both sides of conscience alley should be given a practice run with no one moving through the alley. This will help with voice level, pitch, tone and words.

Model this for the children. You should select one or two statements to persuade the family to stay, for example, *Stay because your friends are here*; *Stay because your home is here*; *Stay because it's safe.* Say the statements in different ways. The first might be too loud, bland and not persuasive, too high-pitched and with too many words. Ask the children to identify what was wrong. Then model it correctly with a whispered but expressive voice, a low pitch and words that are persuasive and repeated.

It would be advisable to allow the whole family to move together through the alley first. Then each family member should move through in turn and finally the whole family again. This will allow plenty of practice and avoid children feeling too self-conscious. It also lets each family member make his/her own choice of action before coming together as a family to decide on whether to settle or move on. The final act is for the family to give their decision after discussion.

The children can now relax and come out of role. It can be worthwhile giving the children the opportunity to talk about what it felt like being in role.

Simplifying the activity
■ You could lead the Viking family or be first to demonstrate going down the conscience alley.

Extending the activity
■ Children could tape-record their suggestions and play the tapes instead of forming a physical 'alley'.
■ Children might like to suggest other situations to explore in a conscience alley.

Linked to
The National Curriculum
for geography, Key Stage 2,
'Improving the environment';
Scottish environmental studies
5–14 guidelines, social subjects,
'People and place'

Our environment

Activity	speaking	listening	group discussion	drama
1. Evaluating our environment photocopiable page 110	▌ speak audibly and clearly	▌ respond to others ▌ identify gist/key points	▌ make relevant contributions ▌ qualify or justify ▌ deal politely with opposing views ▌ explore ideas and evaluate contributions	
2. Reporting back photocopiable page 111	▌ show shape and organisation ▌ speak audibly and clearly ▌ gain and maintain the response of different audiences	▌ ask relevant questions ▌ respond to others	▌ make relevant contributions ▌ qualify or justify ▌ deal politely with opposing views ▌ help the group to move forward	
3. What action to take? photocopiable page 112		▌ recall and re-present important features ▌ respond to others ▌ identify gist/key points	▌ make relevant contributions ▌ qualify or justify ▌ explore ideas and evaluate contributions ▌ help the group to move forward	
4. Action	▌ show shape and organisation ▌ speak audibly and clearly ▌ choose material that is relevant ▌ gain and maintain the response of different audiences	▌ respond to others ▌ identify gist/key points	▌ make relevant contributions ▌ qualify or justify ▌ deal politely with opposing views ▌ help the group to move forward	

Evaluating our environment

Background information
This activity gives children the opportunity to select and devise questions to help them evaluate aspects of their own school environment. They will work in groups of four to focus on one area, making suggestions and coming to a group consensus.

What to do
Ask the children what they understand by the word *environment*. They may suggest a place where people, plants or animals live or they may mention weather conditions. Ask a child to look it up in the dictionary. One definition could be external conditions or surroundings in which people, plants or animals live. Another could be the natural world of land, sea, air, plants and animals.

Explore some examples: *Would we call the park an environment? Does it fit the definition? What about the desert? The North Sea?* Can the children name any environments? They may suggest rainforests, deserts, oceans, the countryside, the seashore, towns. Note responses on the board. Try to group them under the headings *Distant or world, British, Local* and *School*. Categorise their initial suggestions. The park would fit under *Local*, the desert under *Distant or world* and the North Sea possibly under *British*. Encourage the children to consider other environments which fit under each of the four headings. *Is the environment here and where you go on holiday the same? Is the environment the same where each of you live? Do we as a class share any environments? Are there different environments in Britain? How would we categorise the playground as an environment?*

Encourage the children to explain their answers. For example, they might suggest the seashore as an environment. It is a place where people, plants and animals live. Where could it be categorised? Eva says *British* and explains that she has been to St Andrews and Brighton and they are both in Britain and have seashores and beaches. Sam says *Distant/ world* and explains that he has been to Puerto Pollenca in Majorca and Praia D'Oro in Portugal and they both have lovely beaches and seashores. Can they both be correct? Explain to the children that they can, because similar environments can exist in different parts of the world, so we could put *seashore* under both categories.

Now tell the class that they are going to spend a series of lessons working on the environment of the school. They will work in groups of four on one area per group. Focus on the list of suggestions already made under the *School* environment

Objectives
▌ To contribute relevant suggestions audibly and clearly

▌ To justify suggestions

▌ To respond to others' suggestions and reach a group decision

You will need
▌ Photocopiable page 110

Activity time
1 hour 15 minutes

Assessment
▌ Did children contribute?

▌ Were their suggestions relevant and expressed audibly and clearly?

▌ Did they justify their suggestions?

▌ Did they respond to the suggestions of others and reach a consensus?

heading. Can the children suggest other parts of the school to add to the list? The final list will probably include the classroom, playground, gym, dining hall, school entrance, toilets, library, corridors, offices. Explain that in their groups they are going to evaluate how good an area is and if it could be improved. In order to do this they will help to design an evaluation form by selecting appropriate questions from photocopiable page 110. This will help them decide what to look at and how in order to make this judgement.

Take an example – the school entrance – and model this with the children: *If I were a visitor to the school, what would be important about the entrance?* Take ideas from the children, for example it should be clear where to go; it should be bright and welcoming; people should be smiling; the entrance should be secure. Explore the questions on photocopiable page 110, identifying those most appropriate to the entrance example. *Let's think about the entrance hall and try to select the best five questions to evaluate it. Is it bright, clean and attractive? Would this be important for the entrance hall? Yes. Why? Anna says because it's important that people see the school is nice as soon as they come in. Are notices and displays clear, attractive and interesting? Would this be important for the entrance hall? Yes. Why? Ibrahim says because visitors need to know where to go and it is important that everything looks nice. It shows that we care.* You could repeat this process until all questions have been explored.

This would also be a suitable time to explore how the group will come to a consensus if there are more than five suitable points. Explain that the group will have to look at each again and make a case for selecting one over another.

Allocate each group a different area of the school environment. Ask them to discuss and select the five most appropriate questions for that area. They may suggest questions other than those on photocopiable page 110 if they wish. Explore how they might go about this. They could, for example, take each question in turn, discuss its relevance and importance and agree to keep or discard it. Remind the children that everyone in the group will have an opinion that should be considered. If conflict arises about decisions, the group must choose the best way forward through discussion and persuasion or by a vote.

Once the group have agreed on the questions they should cut them out and glue them onto a separate piece of paper to make an evaluation form. Tell them to leave enough space between questions in order to record their findings later. These forms will be used in the next activity to evaluate the areas.

Simplifying the activity
■ Some groups may benefit from adult support when deciding on the best questions.

Extending the activity
■ More able children may prefer to generate their own questions.

Reporting back

Background information
This activity allows the children to use the evaluation forms created during the previous activity. They work in the same groups of four, visiting their allocated area and evaluating it. They then prepare and deliver a report on their findings.

What to do

Explain to the groups that they are going to visit their allocated area of the school environment to evaluate it using their forms. If you feel it is necessary you may like to model this, using the classroom as an example.

Explain that the members of each group have to work together to decide on the answer to each question on their form and to make a suitable comment to explain their answer. For example, for the corridor the group may decide it is too noisy therefore tick or write *Yes* in answer to this question. They may then wish to comment, *At playtimes the corridors are too noisy because everybody is moving at once and talking loudly.*

Each group will then visit its allocated area to observe, answer and record comments on the questions. Give each group a clipboard and pencil and 20 to 30 minutes to complete the evaluation and return to class. If a group is evaluating the toilets you may want to send an adult with them! It may also be sensible to evaluate areas at different times of the day. Make it clear to the children that everyone in the group must give their opinion on the question and be able to explain why. Everyone else must listen and may ask questions. After the discussion on each question the group must agree on their response and reasons. Some children may have to compromise or may be persuaded by another's argument. This is to be encouraged where appropriate.

Check that all groups have returned to the class with the information they need. This might be an appropriate time to reflect on how they worked as a group. Explore this by questioning each group: *Damien, did everyone in your group contribute their opinion? Zara, what about your group, did everyone listen to each other? Did everyone explain their opinion? How did the group reach agreement? Did you vote? Did someone give in to pressure? Was someone persuaded by a good argument? Did one person's opinion dominate?* Next time the groups work together it is worth reminding them of these points.

Objectives
▌ To justify opinions, listen to others and reach a consensus as a group

▌ To prepare and present a report that shows shape and organisation

▌ To present audibly and clearly to an audience

You will need
▌ Evaluation forms created in the previous activity

▌ Photocopiable page 111

▌ One clipboard per group

Activity time
2 hours

Assessment
▌ Did children justify their opinions, listen to others and reach a consensus?

▌ Did they contribute to the preparation of the report?

▌ Did they report back audibly and clearly?

Explain to the groups that you now want them to prepare an oral report on their evaluation to be made to the rest of the class. Remind the children of the key aspects of reporting orally – using a good, clear voice with suitable expression and pace. Model a good and poor example and encourage the children to pull out the good bits. Also remind them that keeping the report relevant and to the point and not giving irrelevant, uninteresting or simply too much detail is important. Again, modelling examples would support the children in this type of presentation.

Introduce and explain photocopiable page 111. The group should record which area they evaluated, which aspects they thought were good, which aspects they thought could be improved and how. Explain that the report will consist of:
1. Reading their questions and responses from the evaluation forms.
2. Reporting those aspects they thought were good from photocopiable page 111.
3. Reporting those aspects they thought could be improved from photocopiable page 111.
4. Reporting their ideas for improving these aspects from photocopiable page 111.

The report could be shared, with each group member taking responsibility for one part. This would give all the children the opportunity to present. Give the groups 30 minutes to prepare the report presentation. This will give time for the children to practise and rehearse and will allow you to support groups and individuals. Give each group five to ten minutes to present their report. These could be presented at different times if preferred.

Simplifying the activity
■ Some groups may require support on the visit to their allocated area to record their comments. They may also need support to read photocopiable page 111 and record their responses.

Extending the activity
■ Some children could be given more freedom to decide on how to report their findings.

What action to take?

Background information
The groups use the information gathered on photocopiable page 111 in the previous activity to consider the range of possible actions for improvement and decide on the most appropriate.

What to do
In preparation for this activity you will need to prepare an OHT or poster pulling together all the areas and aspects identified by the groups on photocopiable page 111 as in need of improvement, for example:

Playground	Classroom	Toilets	Entrance
litter		dull colours	
bumpy surface		smelly	
nothing to do		no soap	

Introduce the poster and explore with the children any common patterns running through the responses. Are all groups identifying the need for better notices and signing? Are most groups commenting on the need to be tidier and cleaner? Recall the children's initial ideas for action on photocopiable page 111 by getting one child from each group to read the ideas for improvement again.

Objectives
▌ To make relevant suggestions based on their evaluations and experiences

▌ To contribute their own ideas during class discussion

▌ To listen and respond to each other's ideas

▌ To discuss, select and justify the most appropriate action, reaching consensus in the group

You will need
▌ Poster/OHT displaying aspects for improvement identified by each group (see 'What to do')

▌ Photocopiable page 111 from the previous activity

▌ Photocopiable page 112

Activity time
1 hour 30 minutes

Assessment
▌ Did children make relevant suggestions?

▌ Did they contribute ideas during class discussion?

▌ Did they listen and respond to the ideas of others?

▌ Did they select and justify actions and reach a consensus?

Explain to the class that in order to change or improve things, people have to take action. Sometimes this action is indirect and involves asking other people to do something. Sometimes it is direct and involves individuals doing something themselves. Explore the different kinds of action it is possible to take. Model an example: *If we identified that the toilets were very gloomy and needed painting what action could we take?* The children may suggest painting them themselves; asking the janitor to paint them; asking parents to paint them; writing to the headteacher to ask for permission to paint them.

You may wish to explain that in many situations you cannot just do whatever you want to do, but have to go through the proper channels. Take the opportunity to explore the relevance of the children's ideas and weigh up possible suggestions. Encourage the children to consider which is the most appropriate suggestion by examining the pros and cons of each. This will help model one way of reaching a consensus. For example: *If we decided to paint it ourselves what would be the advantages/ the pros? It could be done quickly. We could choose the colour. We would feel good when it was finished. What would be the disadvantages/the cons? It would cost us money. It would take time away from our school work. We don't have the painting and decorating skills needed. It might end up a mess. Would it be a better solution to write to the headteacher to ask for the toilets to be painted?* Again explore the pros and cons. This will support the children in their discussions.

Introduce photocopiable page 112 which lists possible courses of action. Read this over with the children to ensure they understand the range of possibilities. Explain to each group that they should take each aspect for improvement identified on their copy of photocopiable page 111 and consider all possible courses of action using photocopiable page 112, then decide on the most appropriate. Tell them you will be listening to them making suggestions and justifying them with reasons, responding to others' suggestions and coming to a group consensus.

They should summarise their decisions on a separate piece of paper – this will become the group's action plan. The plan should include the area they investigated, the aspects of that area they evaluated as in need of improvement, and their suggested action.

Simplifying the activity
■ Provide an action-plan framework for the children to complete.

Extending the activity
■ More able children may wish to compile their own list of ideas for improvement action.

Action

Background information
This final activity allows the groups to select one point from their action plan, brainstorm how to go about the task, then take the appropriate action.

What to do

The children will start in their groups of four. Make sure they have their action plans. Explain that as a group they should decide which action point to work on first. Each group member should decide this for themselves at first and be willing to explain why. Give the groups five minutes to consider everyone's opinion, listen to reasons and decide on the best course of action for the group. Before they do this, you could model an example. A group could be working on the playground as an area to be improved. Two suggestions for improvement are: *Have more bins* and *Have more for people to do in the playground.* Ask: *If we had to decide which of these to work on first, how would we decide?* Suggest that it might be best for everyone in the group to make their own choice and be able to give good reasons why. Jason might say *more bins* because it could be quick and easy to achieve. Helen might say *more to do* because everyone would be happier in the end. Again, encourage the children to give their opinions and consider the pros and cons of each suggestion before coming to a group decision.

Bring the class together and encourage each group in turn to tell the others which improvement point they are working on for which area and the action they have decided to take.

The next part of this activity depends on what action each group has decided to take. Explain that you have set aside 45 minutes to put ideas into action. Each group will have to decide who will do what, make a list of the resources they will need and ensure that these are available. Model this: *My group wants to act on litter in the corridor. The action decided is to put up posters encouraging people to use the bins. What would my group have to consider? For example, how many posters do we need? Who will design and produce them? What resources do we need? Are these resources available?* The group would then go on to complete the posters and display them in the corridor areas.

Set the groups to work independently. Circulate around the room, giving support as required. The children should recognise this as a real activity, so whatever they produce should be used: posters made, letters sent, talks prepared and carried out and so on.

Simplifying the activity

- Allocate group members to each task.

Extending the activity

- Some groups could structure and complete the task independently.

Objectives
- To give an opinion and justify it
- To reach a consensus
- To report their plan to the class
- To make an agreed plan, share out the tasks fairly and carry the plan through

You will need
- Action plans compiled in the previous activity

Activity time
1 hour 30 minutes

Assessment
- Did children give an opinion and justify it?
- Did they reach a consensus?
- How well did they report their plan?
- Did they work together to plan and carry out their task?

How to evaluate our environment

Is it bright, clean and attractive? ☐

Are notices and displays clear, attractive and interesting? ☐

Is it too noisy? ☐

Do you feel safe and secure here? ☐

Is it welcoming? ☐

Is it littered and dirty? ☐

Is it a suitable temperature? ☐

Are the people friendly and approachable? ☐

Is there enough to do to keep busy? ☐

Is it clear where to go? ☐

Is everything you need there for you? ☐

Are there people to ask for help? ☐

Preparing the report

We evaluated _____.

We agreed that these aspects of our area were good:

∎

∎

∎

∎

We agreed that these aspects of our area could be improved:

∎

∎

∎

We had some ideas on how to improve our area:

∎

∎

∎

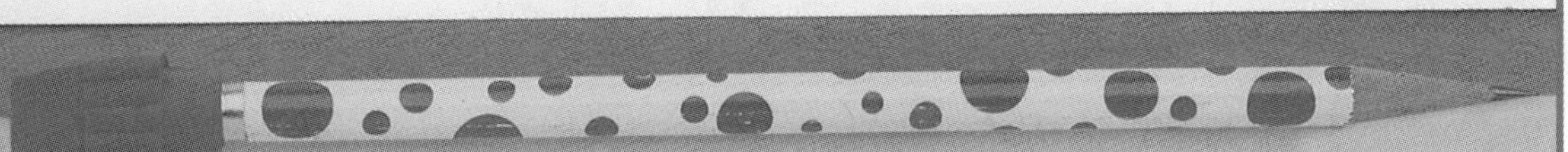

SCHOLASTIC

Ideas for action

■ Write a letter to find out information.

■ Write a letter to give information.

■ Write a letter to ask for help and support.

■ Make a poster.

■ Make notices.

■ Start a campaign.

■ Start a petition.

■ Set down and display rules.

■ Give a talk at assembly.

■ Speak to other classes.

■ Set up a pupil council.

■ Start a playground or corridor patrol.

■ Speak to school staff.

■ Set up an action brigade.

■

■

Chocolate bars

Linked to
The National Literacy Strategy
Framework for Teaching, 'Persuasive writing: adverts';
Scottish English language 5–14 guidelines, 'Talking to convey, information, instructions and directions'

Activity	speaking	listening	group discussion	drama
1. Chocolate bar choices photocopiable page 122		▌ ask relevant questions ▌ respond to others	▌ make relevant contributions ▌ qualify or justify ▌ deal politely with opposing views ▌ help the group to move forward	
2. Presenting the product photocopiable pages 123 and 124	▌ show shape and organisation ▌ speak audibly and clearly ▌ choose material that is relevant ▌ use appropriate vocabulary and syntax	▌ respond to others	▌ make relevant contributions ▌ explore ideas and evaluate contributions	▌ evaluate contributions ▌ create, adapt and sustain different roles ▌ use character, action and narrative to convey ideas
3. Cookery demonstration photocopiable pages 125 and 126	▌ show shape and organisation ▌ speak audibly and clearly ▌ use appropriate vocabulary and syntax ▌ evaluate speech ▌ gain and maintain the response of different audiences		▌ qualify or justify ▌ deal politely with opposing views ▌ explore ideas and evaluate contributions	
4. Chocolate bar advertisement photocopiable pages 127 and 128	▌ use appropriate vocabulary and syntax	▌ recall and re-present important features ▌ respond to others		▌ explore characters and issues ▌ use character, action and narrative to convey ideas

Chocolate bar choices

Objectives
▌ To accommodate different views

▌ To reach a consensus

You will need
▌ A selection of dried fruit, cereals and chocolate

▌ Mixing bowls, baking trays, spoons

▌ Photocopiable page 122

Activity time
1 hour

Assessment
▌ Were children able to accommodate different views?

▌ How successfully did children use the strategies suggested to reach a consensus?

Background information
This first activity provides the springboard for the others in this unit. As children will be involved in making a food item it would be satisfying for them to sell it, for example at the tuck shop or a bake sale. It is not always easy for children to accommodate different views and reach a consensus, and this activity provides them with further experience in these skills. The modelling of related behaviours and language will support children in the selection of ingredients for the chocolate bar and in choosing a name for it.

What to do
Tell the children that a confectionery company want to launch a new chocolate bar. Read this 'advert':

Organise the children into groups of four, explaining that each group is going to make their own chocolate bar, but first will need to decide on the ingredients to include. Display the list of ingredients available to the children and explain that they must choose one ingredient from each of the three categories, for example:

> **Are you imaginative? Can you work with others?**
>
> **Do you loooooove chocolate?**
>
> **If the answer is YES then why not create a new chocolate bar for our expanding company?**
>
> **ALL ideas will be considered!**

Chocolate	Cereal	Dried fruit
milk	puffed rice	apricots
white	corn flakes	raisins
dark	chocolate puffed rice	cherries

Discuss ways in which the groups should handle different views. Prompt them with the following suggestions: *I think we should use ___ because… Does anyone agree? Does anyone have a different idea? Tell us again why you don't agree with Kate's choice. Why don't we take Anil's suggestion for the ___ and Alex's suggestion for the ___, as these were the ones most of us agreed on.* Allow the groups 15 minutes to make their choices. This part of the activity can be undertaken by the whole class in groups at the same time. Thereafter, groups should work with an adult to make their chocolate bars using the three ingredients chosen. In terms of the supervision required, it is anticipated that one or two groups will undertake this at a time.

Once each group has made their chocolate bar, tell the children that they have to decide on a name for their creation. A recap on the impact of alliteration and deliberate misspellings in product/company names could usefully be undertaken at this point, for example *Monster Munch, Kwik Fit. KitKat*. Demonstrate to the class how to use the name-choice slide, constructed from photocopiable page 122. At the same time, model some of the language that might help children to reach a consensus about the name of the chocolate bar, for example *I like ___ because… What about taking Sean's idea for the first part and Carol's idea for the second part? I think John's suggestion about only having one part to the name is good because… Let's look again at our three best ideas so far. Are we all agreed then that …?* Put the children back into groups and issue each group with the name slide. Depending on the ability of the children, you wish to provide them with pre-made slides. Otherwise, let the children make them themselves. Before groups begin to work on a name, remind them that the chocolate bar can have one or two parts to its name and that it might link in some way to the ingredients contained in it.

Bring the class together once names have been decided and collate and discuss the ideas.

Simplifying the activity

■ Tell children the name should have two parts to it, that is, they should choose from both slides.

Extending the activity

■ Ask the children to add their own name ideas to the bottom spaces on the slides.

Presenting the product

Objectives
▌ To recognise how situations can be approached from different viewpoints

▌ To discuss the effectiveness of communication in own and others' work

You will need
▌ Photocopiable pages 123 and 124

Activity time
1 hour

Assessment
▌ Were children able to adopt roles to portray a situation from different viewpoints?

▌ Did children discuss the effectiveness of the communication?

Background information
This activity provides children with an opportunity either to present or evaluate a product through role-play. Although the organisation suggested may initially appear complicated, it should be reasonably straightforward to implement and has been done in this way to maximise involvement. Decisions about how 'spontaneous' the role-play should be and the extent of each group's preparation for it will be dependent on the children's experience of this type of activity.

What to do
The children should remain in their groups from the last activity. Nominate one child from each group to act as a member of the board of directors for the confectionery company. Explain to the children that the remaining members of each group will try to convince the board of directors to accept their chocolate bar idea.

Issue the 'considerations' questions on photocopiable pages 123 and 124 to the appropriate groups. Draw the children's attention to the idea of *audience awareness* when they are preparing questions and contributions to help them adopt an appropriately formal register.

Give time for the board of directors to prepare their questions and for groups to prepare their presentations. One of the first things that should be done is for the board to issue a letter similar to the example on the left to each of the presenting groups.

Once groups have decided on what they will say and who will say it, the focus should shift to *how* questions will be asked and *how* information will be presented. Demonstrate how, through posture, eye contact and tone of voice, different personas can be portrayed. For example, a more nervous presenter might not be making eye contact with others, but a more confident presenter might be able to scan round the group they are speaking to.

Next, direct the groups to undertake their presentations at the allotted time. After each group has made their presentation, give the board time to reach a decision. While the board are in discussion, review the effectiveness of communication with the presenting groups. For example, were they able to maintain a confident stance? Could they have spoken more slowly/quickly/clearly? What did they do to avoid

Dear _____

The Deluxe Chocolate Company invites you to make your presentation for your new chocolate bar to our board of directors on _____ at _____am/pm in room ____. You will be allocated 5 minutes to convince the board why we should choose your chocolate bar. The board is looking forward to your presentation.

Yours sincerely

_____
Chairperson of the board

feeling nervous? Would they change anything they did? Then invite the children to make constructive comments about the effectiveness of communication of the board. For example, Did they welcome groups warmly? Were they able to maintain eye contact as they listened to contributions? Was the tone of their voice appropriate for the situation?

Ask the board to provide feedback by outlining one thing they particularly liked about each presentation, before announcing their final decision.

Alternative organisation for larger classes

Create two boards – Board A and Board B – for the confectionery company and allocate nominated children in such a way that there are three to four board members on each of the two boards. Half the groups in the class will make their presentation to Board A and the other half to Board B. It would be helpful if this was organised in such a way that no board member listens to the presentation from their original group.

Simplifying the activity

■ Give children more guidance on what they might include in their presentation to allow them to focus more on how they will present it.

Extending the activity

■ Ask the groups who are listening to the presentations to make notes or 'grade' the posture, eye contact, tone of voice and so on which could feed into the board's discussion.

Cookery demonstration

Objectives
▌ To give an oral presentation using appropriate linking phrases

▌ To listen to and assess, using given criteria, a mock presentation

▌ To take notes for use during a presentation

You will need
▌ Photocopiable pages 125 and 126

▌ Short video clip of cookery programme (optional)

▌ Video camera (optional)

Activity time
1 hour (more if making the recipes)

Assessment
▌ Did children make good use of the linking phrases? How far did they adapt these?

▌ Did children assess the mock presentation appropriately?

▌ Could children make sense of the notes they took?

Background information
This activity involves children in making a presentation, in the style of a cookery programme, of how they made their chocolate bar (see page 14). It can be adapted to include the use of a video or may be kept as simple as one group performing to another. If you have a willing classroom assistant and a video camera, the former option is to be recommended as it will lend the presentation a more realistic context and also be used afterwards to help children assess their speaking.

What to do
After children have made their chocolate bars tell them that they will shortly be showing others how they did this. Ask them if they have ever watched a television cookery programme. (If feasible, you may want to show a short video clip of one of these programmes to enthuse children and to set the scene for their presentation.) Discuss with the children the components of such a programme, for example introduction, display of ingredients and utensils, demonstration and commentary of each step, final display of finished product and conclusion. Noting these stages on the board might be useful. Draw the children's attention to the pacing of such demonstrations, pointing out that they are deliberately slow to allow the audience time to take notes.

Put the children into the groups they were in for the first activity and ask them to condense their recipe into no more than six steps. This will help the children to be succinct. Some children may find it helpful to draw these steps. Decide whether the presentation/s will involve actually making the chocolate bar or whether the children will simply talk through the steps, using the ingredients, utensils and finished products as props.

Issue photocopiable page 125 to each group. As the focus is on the children's presentational speaking skills, this sheet has been designed to allow children to move to the rehearsals quickly rather than spending time devising a script from scratch. However, the purpose here is to guide, not to dictate, so stress that you will be looking for groups to mix, match, adapt and add to these phrases to make their presentation special to them.

Once children have decided upon the phrases that they will use and have filled in the details of their recipe they should consider the actual presentation. Who will undertake the demonstration? Should this same person also undertake the commentary or will one person commentate while another demonstrates? You may want to make these decisions for the children. Much will depend on the children's levels of confidence and previous experience of presenting.

At this point it might be best to review the features of effective presentations. You could do this by simply going over the rules of speaking clearly and slowly, reminding children to look at the audience, to scan the audience and to take their time when demonstrating the steps. You may want to undertake a mock demonstration and ask the children to use photocopiable page 126 to grade you accordingly. You can decide which parts you will undertake well and which you will undertake less well in order to make the points! Children may want to use this photocopiable sheet during their own rehearsals.

Children will now need time to rehearse and you may want to circulate offering advice and praise, perhaps using the categories on photocopiable page 126 to guide you. If using a video camera, you can decide whether all groups will be filmed, and whether this is to be done one after the other or throughout the week. However, you may wish to keep this activity low key and simply ask groups to present to the class. This would offer children a natural opportunity to listen in order to take notes for their personal use. The true proof of the effectiveness of such notes could be in making the chocolate bars!

Simplifying the activity

■ Ask each group to present to only one other group.

Extending the activity

■ If this activity coincides with a school fête or similar event, it might be fun to set up the video to run at a stall. Of course, live presentations can also take place during such events.

Chocolate bar advertisement

Objectives
▌ To justify opinions by referring to points from discussion

▌ To respond to others' opinions politely and attempt to adapt own ideas accordingly

▌ To use appropriate linguistic devices (eg puns, alliteration) in their adverts

▌ To present adverts in a tone that is in keeping with the message

You will need
▌ Photocopiable pages 127 and 128

▌ A tape of current radio/TV jingles and slogans (optional)

Activity time
1 hour

Assessment
▌ Did children refer to points from discussion when justifying opinions?

▌ Did children use any of the linguistic features discussed?

▌ Did they make use of suggested comments to help them to listen and adapt their own ideas?

▌ Was the tone of the presentation in tune with the message?

> **Background information**
> This activity involves children devising their own slogan and introduction for a radio commercial advertising the chocolate bars created in the first activity. This will give them further practice in justifying their opinions and listening to others in order to come to a group decision.

What to do
In the week before undertaking this activity, it might be a good idea to ask children to note any commercial slogans and jingles that they like. They might also like to ask parents and carers about their favourites. If time permits, you could also tape a few of your favourites or those you find particularly effective to share with the children.

Start the activity by discussing favourite slogans and note some of these on the board. Draw children's attention to the common linguistic features of these slogans, for example the use of rhyme, puns, alliteration, imagery, the limited number of words. Ask children why they think the advertisers normally make slogans short and memorable.

Tell the children that they are going to devise a radio advertisement complete with slogan for their named chocolate bars. Organise the children into their original groups and issue photocopiable page 127. Explain that they should talk about each advertising slogan to decide what they liked and disliked about each one. Encourage the children to make extended comments here and tell them that they cannot simply say, *I like/don't like that one*. You can demonstrate this by indicating what you don't like about the first on: it is too long and doesn't use rhyme, alliteration or puns to help you remember the product; it is bland. You can also add that you *do*, however, like the phrase *every mouthful* and that you may use this in your own slogan later.

Remind children that sometimes we don't initially like something until we hear what others think then we can see the joke or be made more aware of the rhyme or some other aspect. It is therefore very important to listen to others' views here. Tell children that you'd like to hear them responding appropriately by saying things like, *Oh yes, now I see*

what you like about it or *I've changed my mind and agree with Libby now that I can see the joke* or *Now that I've heard you say it out loud I do like the sound of that slogan.* The groups should then agree on the slogan they like best and that fits the name of their chocolate bar. Remind them that they cannot simply use this slogan as it stands; they must make some change to it (or amalgamate it with another) to make it suit their product. At this point it might be helpful to circulate around the groups, encouraging them to be prepared to justify their choices and to refer to some of the linguistic features. Nominate one scribe in each group to complete the photocopiable sheet.

Inform the children that a good slogan is at the heart of a good advertisement, but that a little introduction is normally needed as well. Read the first item on photocopiable page 128 and discuss how it tries to set the scene for listeners and draws upon a common experience. Tell the children that the slogan should end the advert so that it stays in the listeners' minds. What kind of slogan might be appropriate for the first introduction on photocopiable page 128? (Perhaps one that refers to or implies speed, liveliness, action, awakenings.)

Now issue groups with photocopiable page 128 and ask them to decide which of these might best suit their slogan. Encourage them to adapt, add and mix sentences to arrive at a suitable introduction for their slogan. This might best be done by underlining or highlighting words and phrases from all the introductions that are appropriate to their slogan, then arranging these in a way that pleases.

When the children have done this they will be ready to practise reading their adverts. This might be undertaken at times staggered throughout the week to allow you or a classroom assistant time to listen and respond to children's ideas about how the adverts should be read, for example quickly and urgently or quietly and slowly, to reflect the message. You may want to decide who should read the introduction and who should read the slogan. Time must be given to allow children to experiment before recording their adverts on tape.

Simplifying the activity
■ Offer fewer choices of slogans and/or introductions.
■ Let children use their chosen slogan as it is given, without trying to make changes.

Extending the activity
■ Ask children to devise their own slogan that uses at least two of the features of slogans you have examined.
■ Encourage children to think of appropriate sound effects or music that might enhance their advert.
■ Ask children to devise their own introduction.
■ Play the tape to an audience and after five minutes ask them to try to remember as many slogans as they can. This would give children some feedback on the effectiveness of their slogans and on how their advertisements sound.

Chocolate bar name slide

■ Cut out the three strips of paper.

■ Cut along the dotted lines in the bottom strip.

■ Slide the 'name' strips through the dotted lines to make the chocolate bar name slide.

■ Experiment with different combinations.

choco	crunch
milk	cherry
cherry	krisp
apri	choo
fruit	choc
cool	byte

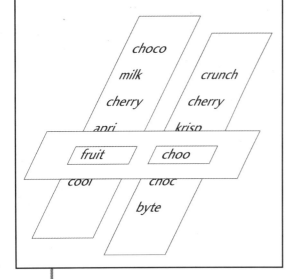

Considerations for the board of directors

	Notes
Who will act as chairperson? Will this change for each presentation?	
How will each group be welcomed? What will you say?	
Who will make notes during the presentations? Will this change for each presentation?	
What questions will you ask about: ▪ the flavour of the chocolate bar ▪ the name of the chocolate bar ▪ who the chocolate bar might appeal to ▪ other questions?	
Who will ask each question? What order will the questions be asked in?	
How will you bring each presentation to an end?	
How will you announce your decision?	

Considerations for the presenters

	Notes
How will you introduce your new chocolate bar?	
What will you say about: ▪ the flavour of the chocolate bar ▪ the name of the chocolate bar ▪ who the chocolate bar might appeal to ▪ other points?	
Who will present different pieces of information? Will there be a lead presenter? Will you all stand/sit?	
Will you use resources to help you, for example photographs, drawings, samples of your chocolate bar?	
How will you finish your presentation?	

Photocopiable

Cookery demonstration

Stage	Possible phrases to use	What we will use
Introduction	▌ Hello. Today's recipe is… ▌ Today we will be making… ▌ Today's recipe could not be simpler. It's called…	
Ingredients	▌ The ingredients you will need are… ▌ Here are the ingredients.	
Utensils	▌ You will need to use… ▌ We have displayed the utensils you need. They are…	
Step 1	▌ First you should… ▌ The first thing to do is… ▌ It's best to start by… ▌ We start this recipe by…	
Steps 2 to 6	▌ Secondly, Thirdly, Fourthly ▌ Next, Now, After that ▌ When you've done that… ▌ You are now ready to… ▌ Finally, Lastly, Last of all	
Conclusion	▌ That's all there is to it! ▌ Enjoy! ▌ Good luck! ▌ Thanks for watching. ▌ Have fun making…	
Some extra phrases	▌ Remember to… ▌ It's a good idea to… ▌ It might be best to…	

SCHOLASTIC

Grading a demonstration

		GRADE
Commentary	Spoke clearly	10 9 8 7 6 5 4 3 2 1 0
	Spoke with appropriate pace	10 9 8 7 6 5 4 3 2 1 0
	Looked at audience	10 9 8 7 6 5 4 3 2 1 0
	Scanned audience	10 9 8 7 6 5 4 3 2 1 0
Demonstration	Took time to show the steps carefully	10 9 8 7 6 5 4 3 2 1 0
	Used the utensils well	10 9 8 7 6 5 4 3 2 1 0
	Smiled at times	10 9 8 7 6 5 4 3 2 1 0
	Recovered from any mistake	10 9 8 7 6 5 4 3 2 1 0
Other?		10 9 8 7 6 5 4 3 2 1 0

Any advice? _____

Chocolate bar slogans

This chocolate bar tastes really nice and you'll enjoy every mouthful of it.

Its chock full of chocolate!

You'll love this chocolate bar. Buy some today.

For the coolest chocolate bar in town try this!

Crunch it! Chew it! Love it!

It's yummy in your tummy!

Let this chocolate bar melt your heart.

If you like chocolate you'll love this!

It's the tastiest treat in town!

Life is sweet when you eat this treat.

It's a real sweet treat!

The advertising phrase we would use would be _____

_____

We chose this because:

 _____

_____

_____

We will change it to suit our chocolate bar by _____

_____

Advert introductions

We know how you feel when you come home from school, tired and hungry and not being able to wait a couple of hours until teatime. That's when you should try Xxxxx. It's the chocolate bar that will make you feel great again and give you the energy to get out there and play until it's time to eat a meal.

Sometimes life seems very loud and rushed and noisy and full of people. Sometimes we just want a few minutes all to ourselves to sit and think and do nothing very much at all. That's when you'll want to slow down and sit down and eat Xxxxx.

When you feel a rumbling in your tummy reach for Xxxxx. It will help you to last until it's time for a proper meal.

Ever suffered from that "Can't wait 'til teatime" feeling? Well, don't worry help is at hand. In fact it's in your local shops NOW. Pop in today and just ask for a Xxxxx. It'll help you beat those hunger pangs!

Sometimes when you feel just not hungry enough for a meal, why not try Xxxxx? It's just the right size to satisfy those "I'm not too hungry but I'd like a sweet" times.

Some chocolate bars are gone in a moment.
Some chocolate bars become quite boring after a while.
Some chocolate bars are just right.
But only one chocolate bars is just perfect.

My little sister loves Xxxxx. My big brother loves Xxxxx. My gran loves Xxxxx. My teacher loves Xxxxx. My chums love Xxxxx. I love Xxxxx. Go on admit it, you love Xxxxx too!

SCHOLASTIC